WRITING
FOR CHILDREN

The Essential Guide

Angela Youngman

First published in Great Britain in 2012 by
Need2Know
Remus House
Coltsfoot Drive
Peterborough
PE2 9BF
Telephone 01733 898103
Fax 01733 313524
www.need2knowbooks.co.uk

Contents

Introduction 5

Chapter 1   Research – Know Your Market 9

Chapter 2   How to Get Started and Get Ideas 21

Chapter 3   Creating Characters 31

Chapter 4   Creating Settings 41

Chapter 5   Developing a Plot 51

Chapter 6   Writing Technique 59

Chapter 7   How to Edit and be Ruthless About Your

Work 69

Chapter 8   Illustrations, Picture and

Games Books 75

Chapter 9   Writing Non-Fiction 83

Chapter 10   Finding an Audience 91

Glossary 107

Help List 109

Introduction

Children's books are by far the most long-lasting type of writing. Everyone has two or three books that they read as children and can always remember. Mentioning the titles immediately brings back memories of a carefree childhood, of happy days and sunlit hours. These are the books that they want to introduce to their own children in due course. Many of these books have become classics in their own right – *Peter Pan, Black Beauty, Alice in Wonderland, The Lion, the Witch and the Wardrobe*. The number of such books is constantly increasing – the arrival of Harry Potter revitalised stories featuring magic and mystery, the gentle worlds of Brambly Hedge and Angelina Ballerina have instant girl appeal, while Alex Rider has become a fixture for many boys in search of adventure.

Talk of huge advances and royalties given to authors like J K Rowling can concentrate the mind of many would-be writers. It seems an easy way of earning a living. Looking along the brimming shelves of any bookshop or library, you can see hundreds of books sometimes only 500 to 1,000 words long. The thought immediately follows – it cannot be that hard to write a book of that length!

In reality, very few fiction writers can write for a living. To most it is a part-time activity combined with a job and/or looking after a family. But that is not a bad thing, as writing just for the money is a poor driver, and tends to create instantly forgettable work.

Not surprisingly, lots of people want to write stories for children. It is said that everyone has a book inside them just waiting to be written – but achieving this is a very different matter. As every would-be writer quickly discovers, writing for children is no easy task. It is not a matter of writing a quick story and having instant success. It is a very, very competitive business. To be a successful children's writer requires talent, persistence, research and some luck in the form of being in the right place at the right time.

'To be a successful children's writer requires talent, persistence, research and some luck in the form of being in the right place at the right time.'

Children are very discerning critics, and are quick to condemn books that they do not like. Their attention span is limited and so a writer has to continually fight to keep their interest. The shorter number of words required for a children's story may seem easily achievable, but in reality it can be very hard to do. Each word has to count. There is no scope for long descriptions. The pace has to match the story, with plenty of tension and good plotting. And, of course, there has to be a satisfactory ending which leaves the reader happy and contented.

It is a market that is constantly growing and offers lots of different opportunities. Whatever your interest, there is a genre to suit. Children's books come in all different shapes and sizes – picture books, puzzle books, short stories, novels, graphic stories, manga, mystery, fantasy, fairy tales, imaginative writing, historical, family and real life, sports, school stories – the list is endless.

So where do you start? Sit down with a sheet of paper or blank document on a computer screen and wait for the words to flow? It can be very discouraging when the words don't come easily and half an hour later, you are still looking at that sheet of paper with perhaps just a few words on it. This can be the most soul-destroying way of writing, especially when you hit a snag or lose the thread of a story. You suddenly find yourself desperately trying to work out what to write next, and are constantly removing or altering words, but not getting anywhere with the story.

If you have long desired to write a children's story but not known where to start, then this is the book for you. Likewise, if you are struggling with the dreaded writer's block – when nothing you write seems to work. Nothing can guarantee publication, but what this book can do is indicate how to create the main elements required for a successful children's book. Good characters, strong plot lines, plenty of tension and action with appropriate settings – and of course, the all-important question which most authors get asked – where do you get your ideas from?

Writing can be frustrating, but fun. As a hobby or part-time career it has lots of advantages.

- There is a wonderful sense of achievement when you reach the end of the story and look back over what you have written.

'Children are very discerning critics, and are quick to condemn books that they do not like.'

Need2Know

- You can leave your own world for a while and enter a different one of your own creation in which anything can happen.

- It keeps the mind alive and alert.

- It opens you up to new experiences while researching or looking for new ideas.

- It does not cost very much – all you need is something on which to write whether it be a computer or old-fashioned pen and paper.

- It can lead to new friends and interests as you talk to others, seek out contacts and find information.

Happy writing!

'Writing can be frustrating, but fun. As a hobby or part-time career it has lots of advantages.'

Chapter One

Research – Know Your Market

Doing your research and knowing your market is a key element in being a successful children's writer. The children's book market is absolutely massive and can provide more opportunities than you ever thought possible. It is not just a matter of writing a story – you need to know which genre or type of story you are targeting, and which publishers are active in a particular market. Not all publishers will cover every type of children's book.

Do not base your knowledge of the children's book market on what you remember reading as a child. While classic stories like *Black Beauty, The Little Mermaid* and *Snow White* are still popular; the market has grown and changed considerably in the way stories are presented as well as the topics covered.

Research

Read as many different types of children's books as you can find. Find out what is being published and what children like to read. Check out the shelves in bookstores and browse among the books. Look at the books the retailers are promoting and identify the different genres. Go and sit in a children's library and watch what children are choosing to read. Talk to librarians and find out about popular types of books.

Go to literary festivals such as those held in Cambridge or Bath each year. This provides an opportunity to listen to authors and study children's reactions to the stories on offer. Try and talk to the authors about their work, and seek their advice in getting started.

'Read as many different types of children's books as you can find. Find out what is being published and what children like to read.'

Seven Stories, the Centre for Children's books in Newcastle Upon Tyne is a very useful place to visit. Housed in a large seven storey building, it contains a bookstore as well as a unique collection of manuscripts and artwork relating to books created in modern Britain. The collection includes work by authors such as Philip Pullman, Robert Westall, Michael Rosen, Jan Ormerod and Ian Mark. There is also a changing collection of exhibitions and programmes, some of which tour the country.

While reading and studying books always ask yourself:

- Why has this book been successful?

- What language is being used?

- What makes this character so appealing?

- How often does the author introduce new surprises into the story?

Checklist

- Read as many children's books as you can.

- Browse the shelves of bookshops and libraries.

- Talk to librarians and authors.

- Visit literary festivals.

- Analyse books and try to work out why they are successful.

Genres and book types

There are many different genres or categories of books. Quite often a book will fit into more than one genre. A book may be science fiction, adventure, mystery; or animals, fantasy, picture book; or fantasy, animals, and historical. Some genres such as love and horror are more applicable to older children and teenagers.

Picture books

Picture books are illustrated in full colour. They are designed for young children and beginner readers. Picture books come in many different forms – early learning, alphabet books, short stories, nursery rhymes, word books, books for reading aloud, books to be looked at, novelty books with lots of lift-the-flap sections, and bath books. *The Mr Men* books and *The Hungry Caterpillar* are among the most well-known books of this type, as are the *Mr Bear* stories.

Novelty books are expensive to produce and are rarely commissioned from a first-time writer. They are usually written in-house.

Most picture book publishers seek to produce co-editions, usually with a US publisher so as to be able to share costs. This makes it more cost-effective and provides a bigger print run.

Historical books

These can cover any historical period, and are common for all age ranges. They frequently involve teenagers or children as heroes and heroines. Explanatory information about customs and historical detail is provided separately in an index at the back of the book. This allows children to follow up queries they may have about events or practices mentioned in the story. While the books are historically accurate, the storyline always takes first place. It combines a mix of adventure, mystery, detection, and for older readers, romance. Typical of this type of book are the *Lady Grace* mysteries. Lady Grace is a maid of honour to Queen Elizabeth I. With the aid of her friends – a laundry girl and a jester – Lady Grace solves all kinds of mysteries including missing treasure, spies and even unexplained deaths.

Alternative history books have always been popular. These are books which are set in a normal period of history, but are changed slightly. A war might have had a different outcome, or there could be magic involved. Typical of these books are Mary Hoffman's *Stravagenza* series set in Venice. Writers generally ask themselves questions like: what if the Nazi's had won the Second World War? What if Napoleon had never come to power? What if Henry Tudor had been killed at the Battle of Bosworth? The answers to these questions can

'Novelty books are expensive to produce and are rarely commissioned from a first-time writer.'

provide material for an alternative history. Historical accuracy remains important for all those parts of the plot which have not been altered. This type of book can offer a lot of opportunities for imaginative work.

Time travel stories are another way of mixing elements of the past, present and future. Characters may start in our world and move backwards or forwards in time, encountering historical characters and playing a part in major events. For the writer, the task is to identify just how they move through time – is it via magic rings, a time machine or perhaps slipping through holes in space and time? Once in their new location, the time travellers invariably have a task to undertake, perhaps a quest or a mystery to solve before they can return to their own time.

Adventure stories

Enid Blyton is the doyen of children's adventure stories with the *Famous Five* novels, but as you will see from any bookshelf, the world of children's books has moved on and such stories have become dated. Adventure stories which reflect modern life, historical events or the future tend to be much more appealing to children and teenagers. Good examples of these books are Marjorie Blackman's *Hacker,* which deals with computers and a girl's attempt to free her father from prison. *The Hunger Games* by Suzanne Collins is set in a future world. Twelve boys and girls are forced to take part in a live TV show called The Hunger Games. There is one rule – kill or be killed. Sixteen-year-old Katniss Everdeen takes her younger sister's place and is determined to survive.

Many of these books can also be described as thrillers. The *Alex Rider* books by Anthony Horowitz portray a teenage spy constantly battling against villains, even though it could lead to his own death or serious injury.

Mystery books

These can be a mix of adventure, fantasy or any other genre but there is always a puzzle, a mystery involved. Enid Blyton's *Famous Five* books are the most well-known type of mystery books, but the market has changed dramatically since these were written. Current fiction includes young detectives such as Young Sherlock and the fairy-tale detectives in Michael Buckley's *The Sisters Grimm*.

The Sisters Grimm stories are a good example of how fantasy and mystery can mix. The Sisters Grimm live at Ferryport Landing with their grandmother. This is a place where fairy tales and storybook characters like Red Riding Hood, Robin Hood and the Mad Hatter live and work alongside humans. The girls solve mysteries in a modern-day world where Morgan Le Fay may be encountered picking up empty French fry boxes and Mordred visits Burger King and Taco Bell. The girls are helped in their detective work by their granny, Puck and Mr Canis – who finds it difficult to keep his human persona and becomes more like the Big Bad Wolf every day.

Fantasy, magic and science fiction

With novels like *The Lion, the Witch and the Wardrobe*; folk legends and myths; this sector has always had considerable appeal to children. In recent years it has become even more popular due to the Harry Potter phenomenon and the revival of Dr Who. The national curriculum has made myths and legends required reading in English schools for Years 5 and 6. Many authors are now seeking to give fantasy, myths and legends new slants, for example Rick Riordan's *Percy Jackson* stories which involve children of the Roman and Greek Gods trying to cope with the modern world. They have to cope with quests, deal with villains and come to terms with their own special abilities resulting from their birth parents. This might be an ability to control the sea, or to use lightning bolts. *Noughts and Crosses* by Marjorie Blackman is a modern fantasy based on racial issues. Noughts are the white minority, ex-slaves to the Crosses. Groups are not encouraged to integrate – so what happens when two children meet and become friends?

Humour

Humour and comedy has always appealed to children. There are lots of books on the shelves. Francesca Simon's *Horrid Henry* books focus on the activities of two brothers – one perfect, one horrid and determined to get into all kinds of humorous mischief. These have been very popular, selling over 15 million copies.

Comedy can be very hard to write. It is easy to go over the top, or be too subtle so that the humour is lost on the reader. If you are interested in this sector, it is best to study successful books and work out why they have been so successful.

Supernatural/horror

These may involve witches and ghosts at a younger level, for example *Vampirates* by Justin Semper which tells a story of vampires and pirates. Elements of horror are added in for older children and teenagers as in Anthony Horowitz's *Raven's Gate* saga, starring a hero who is chased by devil dogs, an animated dinosaur skeleton, is kidnapped and finds himself about to be sacrificed. People who try to help him die horribly.

Animals and nature

Books which fall into this category may involve stories in which real animals behave in a real way, reflecting their animal natures or where animals become anthropomorphic so that they speak and behave like humans. Typical examples include *Watership Down* by Richard Adams, and the talking animals in C S Lewis' Narnia stories. Animal books are frequently used by authors to show how issues like bullying and death can be dealt with.

Social reality

Most twentieth century writers were middle class so wrote about middle-class children. Some recent writers such as Jacqueline Wilson have sought to redress the balance by writing about children from poor or disadvantaged homes. These social reality stories are semi-educational and loved by many teachers. But the problem with this genre is that many children want to be lifted out of everyday life by fiction, not reminded of it.

Educational books

This is a very large market. The majority of the books are designed for use in schools, but some books, such as puzzle books and graphic books, can cross into general reading. Educational books tend to link into curriculum topics, especially literacy, maths and science.

Story books designed for literacy teaching are very popular. All primary schools use special reading schemes that are designed to ensure that children learn specific words and sounds. Phonics is the accepted form of literacy teaching. It is a method of teaching young children to read by learning the sounds of letter groups, syllables and individual letters.

Reading schemes are aimed at different groups such as:

* Beginner readers – these are simple reading books which are designed to encourage children to read.

* Remedial readers – these are designed for older readers who have difficulty in reading. They may be children who have learning difficulties, or are learning to read at a much slower rate. Stories have to appeal to an older age range, but have language suitable for a younger one, for example a 10-year-old might be reading at the level of a 6 or 8-year-old.

* Support fiction – these are stories which are designed to encourage discussion within the classroom. Typical topics include not talking to strangers, bullying, crossing roads, what to do if you get lost, respect for different religious groups, why you should be kind to animals etc.

What is important to remember when researching this market is that books for reading schemes are written to very rigid rules. Each book has a clearly specified vocabulary that must be used. Specified words are added at each level, building on words learned earlier in the series. Subject matter is equally rigid – all books have to be politically correct and involve a mix of cultures and nationalities. Religious conventions have to be borne in mind and the books are intended to be totally inclusive of all groups. As a result, a story which

'Educational books tend to link into curriculum topics, especially literacy, maths and science.'

involves pigs has to be avoided all costs since these are taboo to Muslims. Stories are generally contemporary, dealing with issues that the children meet in their daily life. Writers are forbidden to use topics like guns, alcohol, knives, occult including witches and wizards, and any religious references.

Series books

Series books may not be immediately obvious when you look on the shelves of booksellers, but they are quite a big market. Created by a publisher rather than a writer, the books are always set in a specific world and have a clearly identifiable group of characters. Lots of different writers will be used to write the stories.

This type of book is worth considering if you are able to work within a very strict boundary. The main company working in this field is Working Partners. They commission authors to write books about various series characters such as *Rainbow Fairies, Animal Ark, Warriors, Beast Quest*. Such series have proved very successful. *Animal Ark* began as a six-book series, and now numbers over 100 titles. *Rainbow Magic* has sold over 5 million books in the UK and elsewhere.

If you want to write for a series, you must do your homework first. Read as many books as possible within a series and get to know the characters. Then make up some stories of your own using those characters and send these to the publisher as examples of your work. If they like them, then they will provide detailed guidelines from which to work. You get a smaller share of the royalties, but you are likely to enjoy high sales.

Teenage

The crossover between older children/teenage/young adult and adult can be very blurred. It is possible to find books which appeal to all these age ranges; the best example being the *Harry Potter* books. Sometimes these books may have a different cover for each readership group. Other well-known crossover books include *Sophie's World* by Jostein Gaarder, *The Boy in the Striped Pyjamas* by John Boyne and Maria Snyder's *Study* series (*Poison Study, Magic Study* and *Fire Study*).

Popular teenage subjects include real-life problems and concerns, vampires, romance, paranormal, gothic, sports, adventure, mystery, war and horror. Book lengths are generally 30,000 words upwards. Research has shown that teenagers choose a book for its storyline, whether it is an author they like, and whether the book cover appeals. Stories targeting this market tend to be told through teenage rather than adult eyes. A young adult character plays a key role in the story.

Checklist

- Use libraries and bookshops to identify books from each category.
- Where do the categories cross and combine?
- Can you identify the age ranges being targeted by each book?

Market opportunities

Look for emerging trends and gaps in what is being published. The publication of the *Harry Potter* stories immediately caused a boost in magic and fantasy tales, while Caroline Lawrence's *Roman Mysteries* led to the development of other historical stories usually in popular curriculum subjects like the Tudors. While there may be few opportunities provided by writing yet more Tudor mysteries, there could be potential in Victorians or the Egyptians.

Consider mixing genres such as a historical fantasy, a science fiction mystery, or a sports adventure. Craig Simpson has created a popular Second World War series for boys which involves war, mystery and adventure. A typical storyline in the series is *Dead or Alive* in which a rogue agent has vanished. Teenage special agents have to enter occupied Europe to bring the agent back, dead or alive.

While researching the various genres, make a note of any publishers working in the areas you are interested in. Remember that publishers do focus on different activities:

- Some concentrate on selling into bookshops.
- Some concentrate on libraries.

'Research has shown that teenagers choose a book for its storyline, whether it is an author they like, and whether the book cover appeals.'

- Some concentrate on educational books – and may not even be listed under children's books.

Consider the length of the various types of books. Which type would you be happier writing? A picture book may only be 300 or 400 words long, while a novel may be 20,000 words or more. *Goodnight Mister Tom* by Michelle Magorian is over 40,000 words long, while *Matilda* by Roald Dahl is just 20,000 words.

Look at the language used in each of the different genre, and consider the age range for which it is aimed. Age distinctions can get very blurred from about 9 to 10 years onwards.

Try writing the outlines of stories for each of the different markets, based on your research. Ultimately, choose the genre in which you wish to work based on what you like. Writing takes time and you need to ensure you are enjoying what you do. If you enjoy the genre, then you will enjoy writing it – if you do not like a genre, then it will be very hard to write it successfully.

'Writing takes, and you need to ensure you are enjoying what you do. If you enjoy the genre, then you will enjoy writing it – if you do not like a genre, then it will be very hard to write it successfully.'

Summing Up

- Study all the different genres available.

- Read widely across all forms of children's literature.

- Practise writing outline stories for different genres.

- Decide which genre suits your style of writing and are of interest to you.

- Identify publishers working in those sectors.

Chapter Two

How to Get Started and Get Ideas

Having decided you want to write – where do you start? Sitting looking at a blank screen and wondering what to write is very hard. Your confidence quickly disappears.

Finding inspiration

Start by looking for inspiration. This can be found all around you, while travelling on public transport, visiting places, museums, art galleries, shops, watching TV, and reading newspapers.

Carry a notebook and pen with you all the time. Jot down scraps of information that seem interesting, snatches of conversation, ideas, ways of speaking, people you see, clothes that are being worn, hairstyles, unusual words, even names of pubs or shops. Jot down descriptions of places you see, take photographs to remind you or buy postcards and place these inside your notebook.

Be observant. Look at the sights and scenes around you and try to describe them. Be constantly aware of your surroundings and look for things which catch your attention. It might be a passing street sign, a mural, an advertising slogan or a headline. Look at the weather each day and build up collections of words or descriptions. References to rain dripping down windowpanes, trees bending in the wind, icicles hanging from house eaves can be used to remind you later when you are writing a story.

Sit in a café, drink coffee and jot down notes about people around you. Ask yourself what sort of job you think they might have, what personal characteristics they display, how they look. Listen to people talking and identify any key phrases they use, as this can be a characteristic method of talking. Someone may be frequently ending a sentence with the words 'I know' or 'I do'.

Don't ignore your other senses. Think about what surfaces are like to touch and jot down the words that come to mind. What do they feel like – smooth, silky, hard, rough, big, small, tiny, miniscule, gritty, textured?

Listen carefully – what sounds can you hear in different locations? A passing reference to a digger churning up a pathway can help bring a scene alive. Think too of smells and tastes. What are they like and are there any comparisons that can be made? In *Alice in Wonderland*, Alice drinks a liquid that has a mixed flavour of various foods including cherry tart, pineapple, toffee, hot buttered toast and custard.

'Always keep a notebook by your bed to write down ideas overnight.'

Always keep a notebook by your bed to write down ideas overnight. Don't leave it until morning to write down ideas and scraps of information. By then the ideas will have been forgotten. Sometimes the best ideas can come when you are relaxing and about to go to sleep or when you are in the shower.

Collect information

Collect information from all sources including travel brochures, theatre programmes, newspaper clippings, and snippets of information. These can be extremely useful in giving ideas, or helping a story to develop. Even Dickens used material of this kind.

The Times, January 14th 1834, reported the case of 10-year-old Edward Trabshaw who ran away from home and met a slightly older boy called John Murphy playing marbles in Regent Street. John Murphy took him to his father's house. This was 'a dark and filthy room' where there were '13 to 14 little girls all miserably clad and huddled together in a corner'. Edward Trabshaw was told to join the children and that he would be beaten or killed unless he returned with some money after a day's thieving. Henry Murphy was described as having 'a countenance in which cunning and ferocity were strongly blended'. He was later charged with 'keeping a place of reception for runaway children for the purpose of compelling them to rob and beg'.

By looking at this newspaper account it is easy to see how Dickens amended it to suit his purposes. John Murphy became the Artful Dodger, and Henry Murphy, Fagin. All the characteristic elements are present – children forced to steal and beg, poverty-stricken surroundings, an old miser and a boy who draws others into the miser's web.

Always be ready to look for unusual incidents or events. Some years ago, there was a story about a digger clearing junk from the bottom of a canal. The digger pulled up a rusty lump of metal and a chain. Then the driver went away for lunch. When he came back, a whirlpool had appeared in the canal and all the water was disappearing down a hole. The reason was simple – he had pulled the plug out. For a writer the story immediately raises questions. Where did the water go? What happened on the other side? Could this be turned into a magical event? Perhaps a water sprite or a monster lived down the hole drinking up all the water? What would happen if the monster escaped from the hole? What might the monster look like? Would he demand food? Would he try to drink up all the water in the world? Perhaps he makes friends with a young boy?

By asking and answering such questions, you can quickly build up a plot line or a series of characters which can then be developed into a story.

Create lists of descriptive words in your notebook. This can help speed up the writing process. You can easily refer back when looking for a suitable word. For example, start with words to describe colours. Anyone can write that a character has green eyes – but you can make the character more alive by saying they are sea green. It immediately creates a specific image in the reader's mind.

Typical lists might be:

Green:

Sea green

Velvet green

Leaf green

Pale green

Mint

Grass green

Blue:

Marine blue

Sea blue

Dark blue

Sky blue

Blue of sailor's trousers

Vivid blue

Navy blue

Aqua

Turquoise

Houses:

Detached

Terraced

Bungalow

Row

Manor house

Flat

Apartment

Transport:

Horse-drawn tram

Car

Bicycle

Penny farthing

Cart

Motorbike

Velocipede

Checklist

▓ Keep notebooks permanently available.

▓ Be a magpie.

▓ Collect ideas, words, descriptions, pictures, photos, postcards.

▓ Remember that research is a continuous process – you can do it wherever you are.

Writing methods

Everyone has a different way of writing. What you have to do is find out what suits you. Find a routine that suits you. Are you happier writing on screen or with a pen and paper? There is no right or wrong way of writing.

Some authors start with a character and create a story about it. A famous example is that of C S Lewis. The idea of a faun standing under a lamp post in a snowy landscape came to his mind first. Asking himself why a faun should be under a lamp post, and why it should be a snowy landscape eventually led to the plot of the classic book *The Lion, the Witch and the Wardrobe*.

Some writers just start to write and see where the story takes them. Lauren Child, author of *The White Giraffe,* says she never has any idea where the story is going when she begins to write. She starts writing and then sees where it leads her.

Arthur Conan Doyle took a very different approach. He started at the end of a story and worked backwards. His *Sherlock Holmes* stories were plotted out after he had worked out the ending.

'Everyone has a different way of writing. What you have to do is find out what suits you.'

Other authors very carefully plot out a story from start to finish. A good example of this is J K Rowling. The idea for her *Harry Potter* books arose during a train journey from Manchester to London. She came up with the idea of a boy who doesn't know he is a wizard, who is sent off to wizard school. Working out from that idea, she asked herself, 'Why doesn't he know he is a wizard?' The rest of the journey was spent creating basic characters and ideas. By the time she reached London, she had created the idea of Hogwarts School of Witchcraft and Wizardry, and had decided that it would be a seven-book series with each book following a year in Harry's life.

Even with that background, writing the books was not instantaneous. She spent five years collecting unusual names, Latin words, outlining histories for groups like the Death Eaters and Dementors, as well as developing detailed back stories about all the characters including each of the key students at Hogwarts with their magical heritage and individual abilities. Apart from using her imagination, she used ideas from folklore and mythology. For example, she looked at stories of mysterious black dogs – in Yorkshire, Black Shuck is known as Padfoot, a black, calf-sized dog. Grindylows are Yorkshire watersprites with long fingers, pointed fangs, while Dobby is a friendly household hobgoblin found in Lancashire.

Checklist

- Are you happier with pen and paper or a computer screen?
- Try each type of writing method.
- Decide which type suits you.

Writer's block

At some point, every writer will encounter the problem of writer's block. It is a horrible moment when you stare at a blank screen or a blank sheet of paper and the words just will not come. The more you try to think about what to write, the worse it becomes, as you desperately try to think of words to say or where to take the story. Don't feel too frustrated or despairing. Every writer experiences this problem. Even J R R Tolkien struggled. He left his characters stuck in The Mines of Moria for a year before finding an answer to their predicament.

Fortunately, there are many techniques that can be used to overcome the problem. The most common ones are:

- Go back to your original chapter notes. Read them through and inspiration may occur.

- Stop writing and have a break. Go for a coffee or go for a walk. A change of scenery often provokes a new idea. But remember to take your notebook so you can jot down anything that comes to mind.

- Listen to a piece of music. Jot down ideas, thoughts it brings to mind. What does the music suggest to you? It may be totally unrelated to what you were trying to write, but the exercise can stimulate the brain.

- Find a picture that is similar to the setting about which you are writing. Look at it and imagine your characters inside that picture. What are they going to do next?

- Work on something totally different – perhaps a plot outline for another story, or try creating a new character. It can throw up new ideas.

- Study your ideas folder. It might stimulate your imagination. Working on something different, even a new plot outline, can bring a new perspective to the piece of work you were originally writing.

- Consider brainstorming with friends, co-writers, children. Don't dismiss any ideas that arise – the next one might be the one you need, and you do not want to discourage future suggestions. You might be able to use those other ideas at some other time.

- Discuss the plot with children. Ask what they think ought to be the next step for the characters. A fresh eye on the plot can make a tremendous difference.

- Outside factors may be posing a problem. There might be disturbances such as workmen digging up a gas main outside your house. This can be distracting and make it difficult to concentrate. Find somewhere else to write for a while, or take a break until the digging has stopped.

- Do something different. Concentrate on doing some research down at the library, sit in a railway station and watch people, noting characteristics such as the way they speak, move or dress, or simple location information.

- You may be trying to work for too long a period. If you are new to writing, it can be very hard work if you try to write for eight or nine hours a day. It may be that you are only really creative for two or three hours. The answer is to break up your writing periods into more manageable chunks. Try and divide time between writing and research so that you always feel you are doing something.

- Check your writing time. It may be that you are more creative in the mornings or evenings than in the afternoon. Just aim to write during those creative times.

- If all else fails, put the story to one side and start something else. Come back to it later. Most writers have unfinished work.

'Get into the habit of writing something every day. Writing is a skill that has to be practised and developed.'

Above all, keep on writing. Do not give up. Practise, practise, practise. Write anything, if necessary just write what comes to mind. Get into the habit of writing something every day. Writing is a skill that has to be practised and developed. Only with practice will your writing skills develop. It is extremely unusual for someone to sit down and write a fantastic story without any preparation at all. Most successful writers will have spent a long time practising their craft before approaching publishers.

Summing Up

- Collect information.

- Have notebooks always available.

- Jot down ideas as they come to you.

- Always be on the look out for ideas, snippets of information and write them down instantly before you forget them!

- Practise, practise, practise your writing.

Chapter Three

Creating Characters

Every story needs a selection of characters – a hero, a baddie, friends and helpers. It is the writer's task to bring these characters to life.

Names

Names should be believable and, if necessary, suited to the time period. Writing a story about a girl named Tracy living in the England of Elizabeth I would not be very believable since the name Tracy did not exist then. Harry Potter is a name to which anyone can relate. It is an ordinary sounding name, nothing special. As such it is the exact opposite to what his character really is. Secondary characters are given more unusual names which encourage them to stand out in the memory of the reader such as Draco Malfoy, Hermione Granger.

A story set in the future might require specially created names – make sure they are understandable and can be pronounced. Children may be reading the book aloud and if they have to keep struggling to pronounce a name, it will dent their confidence.

A book of baby names can be a very useful aid to a writer. Such books often give lists of names according to nationality, or to time periods. They also provide the meanings of names, which can help tailor the name to the character. Phone books are another good source of potential names. Take the first part of a name from one page and a surname from the next page. Think about whether you are choosing a name for a good or a bad character. Evil characters have harsher, sharper names.

Surnames help make characters stand out. Decide whether you want ordinary names that will be immediately familiar to readers, or whether you want to stand out. Adding a hyphen to a surname is a good way of making surnames instantly appear grander e.g. Fotherington-Smythe. Occupations and the names of towns and villages can make very good surnames.

Things to avoid:

- Avoid knowingly choosing the names of real people – this can lead to disputes, especially if the person concerned feels you are damaging their character.

- Avoid using names which are too similar for boys and girls, such as Francis and Frances, as this can confuse the reader.

- Avoid having the same starting letter for several names. Writing a scene in which there is a conversation between Edward and Edmund can lead to confusion, especially among beginner readers.

- Avoid stereotyping. Grannies do not sit in rocking chairs knitting and criminals can be found in every nationality.

Checklist

- Names should be easy to pronounce.

- Names should be believable.

- Don't choose confusing names with similar sounds or spelling.

Developing characters

Think of people you know – they always have rounded personalities, possessing both good and bad points. Your characters must be equally rounded. They need their faults as well as their good points. Look for basic qualities that can make a character stand out. There might be a happy-go-lucky character, who is friendly with a quiet, sensitive girl, and a boy who is always making plans and coming up with lively ideas. Such groups of characters can be seen in everyday life, and it is easy for children to relate to them. The relationship between such characters leads to interesting storylines.

'Avoid knowingly choosing the names of real people – this can lead to disputes, especially if the person concerned feels you are damaging their character.'

Use conflicting characters within a story as this adds interest. For example, one boy could be keen on creating conflicts and likes army life, while another is peace-loving and quiet. One boy could be studious, while another is keen on sport; one character is an introvert, while the other is an extrovert. Always add a touch of unpredictability to the character's development. If the character is a good runner, then let them hurt an ankle. How do they cope? Ask yourself how a situation could get worse for a character – then make those things happen within the storyline.

Each story needs some good and bad characters. There should be a hero (sometimes referred to as the protagonist) and a villain (the antagonist). The antagonist may not necessarily be evil, but is the person who is opposing or in conflict with the protagonist. The antagonist always tries to thwart the hero.

Put all the details about your characters in a separate notebook. These details can be referred to when necessary. It will help you avoid mistakes, for example saying a character has blue eyes in one chapter, only to refer to their green eyes later in the book. It makes editing much easier.

Think about your main characters and really get to know them. Ask yourself questions, for example:

- What is their background?

- How are they educated?

- Where do they live? Town or country?

- What type of house do they live in?

- What do their parents do for a living?

- What are their hobbies?

- What are their good points, bad points?

Answering these questions will help your character's back story come alive, and help make them more believable for your readers. The amount of detail needed will depend on the story. J K Rowling wrote a series of seven epic stories – she spent years creating the back stories and collecting background information on all her characters. You may be dealing with just one short story, so will not need quite as much information.

'Each story needs some good and bad characters. There should be a hero (sometimes referred to as the protagonist) and a villain (the antagonist).'

If your character is from a historical period, make sure that your historical background is correct. Basic historical data should be accurate – it is no use saying that Elizabeth I inherited the throne after her father Henry VIII died. There were three other monarchs between Henry VIII and Elizabeth becoming queen.

Keep the number of characters in any story to manageable levels. Too many characters can easily confuse the reader. You only need a handful of characters. All subsidiary characters act as sounding boards or foils for the main characters. They can provide a way of adding a lighter note or flashes of humour or for bringing a problem to light. You must have a reason for each subsidiary character being in the story.

The type of characters will depend on the genre in which you are working. If you are writing a school story or a story set in the modern world, then it needs to be multicultural and include characters from other nationalities. You can consider updating aspects of characters in literature. For example, ask yourself what would Just William be like nowadays? How could a boy like William from the 1930s be turned into a boy of today? What would his interests be? Who would his friends be? What kind of adventures would he have? What trouble could he become involved in?

In books aimed at younger children, any characters that appear to be in dangerous situations like getting lost, would be better portrayed as animals, fairies or elves rather than children. This sets the child slightly away from the implied danger, and makes it less frightening.

Above all, choose the ages of your characters carefully. The hero should be in the target range of your chosen age group. You can include younger or older siblings or accompanying children, but they should not play as important a role. The hero and any other main children should be at the top of the age range. So if your book is aimed at the 7 to 11 age group, your key characters would be aged around 11 to 12 years old, but have some younger children or siblings about 7 to 8 years old. This helps widen the book's appeal, as younger children have a character to which they can relate.

Checklist

- Keep the number of characters to manageable levels.

- Do not have too many characters.

- Make them believable.
- Characters should have good and bad points.
- Choose character ages to match your readership.

Adults

If you are including adults in the story, ask yourself what type of adults are needed – parents, teachers, an older brother? In the *Just William* books the central characters are three boys and a younger girl. Adult characters are parents, older brothers and sisters. There are occasional references to other adults encountered during the boys' adventures, such as a gamekeeper and Mrs Bott. Conflict is provided by the younger girl's desire to play with the boys, even though this does not fit in with her mother's plans. From being a girly girl, she suddenly becomes scruffy, and mud stained.

Character creation

If you are really struggling trying to create a character, it can help to play a simple game. You will need 1 or 2 dice, plus some lists of character attributes. In the following example I have used fantasy characters, but the lists can be amended to suit characters from any type of genre. All you need to do is create appropriate lists of attributes and allot them numbers from one or more dice. The more tables of options available, the more detailed the character or location becomes. To play, you throw the dice and see what number is revealed. Write down the matching attribute. Successive throws of the dice will steadily develop a character.

For example:

Fantasy people

Race	**Class**
1 Elf	1 Knight
2 Fairy	2 Wizard
3 Human	3 Druid
4 Troll	4 Prince/princess
5 Dwarf	5 Warrior
6 Pixie	6 Thief

Weapon	**Clothing**
1 Sword	1 Steel armour
2 Staff	2 Leather armour
3 Bow and arrow	3 Cloak
4 Battle axe	4 Robes
5 Dagger	5 Flowers
6 Poison	6 Silk

Action	**Emotion**
1 Fighting	1 Angry
2 Hiding	2 Frightened
3 Fleeing	3 Laughing
4 Dying	4 Crying
5 Feasting	5 Peaceful
6 Sleeping	6 Unfriendly

So if you roll Race 4, Class 5, Weapon 6, Clothing 6, Action 2, Emotion 3 the result is a laughing warrior troll, dressed in silk, in hiding and using poison as a weapon. This provides a good basis for developing a character and story to go with it. All you have to do is start expanding it by thinking about how the troll would talk, what he would do, why he was in hiding.

Similar lists can be drawn up for almost any other characteristic or location – to include caves, mountains, sea, unicorns, lions, bears, woods etc. The options are as wide as your imagination.

Another useful exercise in character creation is to think about objects around you. Let your imagination go wild. Look at a broom and think about how it might talk, what type of hairstyle it might have, what would it like to do – go riding through the sky on a moonlit night rather than spending all its time in a corner or brushing up the dirt. Is it lonely? Does it have lots of friends? Then look for a very different type of object which could be made into a character. It could be a handbag or a squeezy bottle. Explore the nature of that object in the same way. What happens when the two characters meet? Perhaps they are both being thrown into the rubbish? Do they make a dash for freedom?

Photographs and pictures can provide useful aids in character development. Look at photographs and see what they can tell you about a person or what you can suggest about them. Always consider the back story – why is the person in that particular setting? It might be a picture of a boy walking sadly beside the sea.

Ask yourself:

- Why is he there?

- Has he lost something or someone?

- Has there been an argument?

- How old is he?

- Is he hurt?

- Does he look lonely?

- What do his clothes suggest about him?

- Is he clean and tidy, fashionable, scruffy, or from a different culture or nationality?
- Could he be an illegal immigrant, a newcomer to the area?
- If he started to speak, what would he sound like?

Character copyright

Do not use other people's characters unless you have permission to do so. You can do fan stories for fan websites, but you cannot publish them anywhere else without permission. Fan stories of this kind can be a good way of practising your writing skills. It can help get your name known, as agents and publishers do look at these websites.

'Do not use other people's characters unless you have permission to do so.'

Sometimes writers are asked to create new stories about well-loved characters – but this is always organised by the people who hold the copyright. Publishers Frederick Warne hold the copyright to the characters within Beatrix Potter's stories. They commissioned Emma Thompson of Nanny McPhee fame, to write an official Peter Rabbit sequel to celebrate the 110th anniversary of the first Beatrix Potter story in 2012. The story takes Peter Rabbit on a journey to Scotland where he meets a gentle giant called Finlay McBurney, a distant Scottish relative. The idea came as a result of Emma's research into Beatrix Potter's childhood holidays in Scotland.

Another example is that of Andrew Lee who has created a series of books entitled *Young Sherlock*. These books take the character of Sherlock Holmes and focus on what he might have been like as a teenage boy. In order to do this, he had to obtain the consent of the Conan Doyle family because they hold the copyright to Conan Doyle's work and character.

Checklist

- Make sure your characters are not subject to copyright.
- Create your own individual characters.

Character development

Throughout the story, characters need to be seen developing. By the end of the book, a character should have grown or decreased in status. They should have learned something from their experiences. A bully might learn to act in a different way, a timid child gains confidence, someone who does not trust, learns to trust. A good example is the character of Edmund in C S Lewis' *The Voyage of the Dawn Treader*. By the end of the story Edmund has learned to be a much better, pleasanter character. No longer a bully, he now works with other children and has found his own personal strengths.

Summing Up

- Make your characters believable.
- Do not copy other people's characters.
- Take care you do not breach any copyright restrictions.
- Show how your characters develop throughout the story.

Chapter Four

Creating Settings

Many writers overlook the setting in which a story is based, regarding it as less important than the characters or the plot. They pay less attention to the location in which a story is set, and refer to it only briefly. This is an error that should be avoided.

The fact is that the setting and location help bring the story alive. As a writer you need to know and understand your setting. If it is real to you, then it will be real to your reader. Remember the example of J K Rowling who spent a long time creating her magical world. She created it in painstaking detail. The result was that from the very first page, her world came alive. Readers could imagine it, and they were actually there experiencing it along with Harry Potter and his friends.

Memorable settings

Begin by looking at how established authors use their settings. Read books and try to identify what setting they are using. Is it countryside or town? Is it a fantasy world or a real world? Are places recognisable? Are real places mentioned – and if so, how are they brought alive?

There are many locations in children's literature which stay permanently in the memory. There is the London nursery where children have a dog for a nanny, the rambling expanse of Toad Hall, the world of Oz with its Emerald City and the Yellow Brick Road. Think too of the House of the Tailor of Gloucester tucked away down a narrow alley; and Wonderland with its rabbit holes, playing card soldiers and white roses painted red.

'The setting and location help bring the story alive. As a writer you need to know and understand your setting.'

A more recent creation is Howl's Moving Castle from the books of Diana Wynne Jones. The castle walks on chicken legs around the countryside. It belches out smoke from the chimneys and has doors which lead into a variety of different worlds and countries.

None of these creations are described in lots of detail covering several long paragraphs. There may be a short description at various points within a story, but the main picture is built up in the reader's mind by a judicious choice of words. Hints may be given about a specific location, sights seen from a window, references to smoky rooms, the noise of a funfair. It is the combination of detail and atmosphere that create an overall impression of a location, for example accounts of Sophie's attempts to clean the castle with its rainbow bathroom and deal with Calcifer the fire demon, who lives in the fireplace.

Checklist

- Which locations do you remember from childhood stories?
- Identify the features which make a location real.
- Look for memorable settings in children's stories.

Real places

If you are writing about a real place which actually exists in the real world, and which children might well visit, it is very important to get the details right. If you are writing about a trip on the London Eye, then you need to make sure you have located it on the correct bank of the River Thames. Do not write that it is next to Big Ben, because that would be incorrect. You will get readers pointing out why you are wrong. Children can be very critical.

If you are writing a non-fiction book, it is even more important to be accurate in your descriptions.

A variation on using a location which actually exists, is to create a location within a modern world. You can use a locality you know, but give it a different name. You can hide its real nature using a variety of names, and invent places such as a village or town which does not exist. This makes it slightly different, and unique to you.

Make sure that your details are accurate. Draw yourself a map to make sure you do not contradict yourself within the book. For example, you might write that the supermarket is beside the railway station. But earlier in the book, you may have referred to John walking a mile to reach the railway station after leaving the supermarket.

Names can be made up or chosen from maps, timetables, natural features like Forestdene or Hillside. When travelling or reading, look out for any unusual eye-catching names like St Necton's Glen, Black Park, Rotherfield Peppard, Toot Balden or Stoke Talmage. Note these down in your notebook for future use.

Historical settings

These locations are the hardest to create. You need to be very, very accurate. It is vitally important to do your research and research in depth. Every detail helps, especially with regard to what people ate and wore, how they entertained themselves, travelled, and the type of hobbies they might have. In the Lady Grace books, the young maid of honour is shown doing blackwork embroidery on the sleeves of her gowns.

You must make sure that you use the correct terms, have characters wearing the correct clothing and living in the correct type of buildings. Do not assume that because ruffs were worn in late Elizabethan times, they were also worn at the start of the reign of Elizabeth I.

As you have chosen to write about a period that has existed, there is lots of information available and readers are likely to pick up on any mistakes that you make.

There is always a danger that a writer can become too fascinated by the detail of a historical period. As a result, there is a risk of incorporating too much detail in a story. Just because you are interested in all the tiny details that you have discovered, do not assume that your reader will be equally interested. The reader can get swamped by the presence of too much information and this can hold up the action, and ultimately bore readers. You do not need to include every detail in your book – just those details which help the plot along, and bring the location to life.

When you write, make sure you are in the mindset of the period. Unless you are writing an alternate history where events are not quite as happened in reality, you do not want to have a medieval lady talking about female emancipation or wanting the vote!

Many writers of historical novels include a short glossary at the back giving explanations of clothing, medicine or household items referred to in the book. This avoids the risk of a child getting bored by too much information. If they are interested and want to know more, the information is immediately available. They can refer to it, yet it does not interrupt the flow of the story.

Checklist

- Do your research.
- Make sure you have accurate information.
- Use detailed information wisely.
- Write down details of any location you visit.

Fantasy worlds

Anything goes in a fantasy world. These worlds are peopled by trolls, dragons, elves, giants, magicians, tree people or made-up creations such as Ruthids, aeromen, leaf children, animated twigs or talking dustbins. Their settings can be equally varied – you might have mountains, trees and rivers but in a world of permanent snow and ice, or just simply be a normal world peopled by fantasy creatures.

Ask yourself what makes your fantasy world special. Is it country or town? Who rules it? Are there wizards, trolls, gnomes, hobgoblins, fairies? What type of people live there – are there talking animals or talking flowers? Think about clothing, lifestyles and houses. What do your characters eat? What are their buildings made of? What is the weather and the climate? Is it a modern setting, pseudo historical, an alternate history, a foreign country, a past world? Think about geographical details – mountains, rivers and towns. What do people do in your fantasy world? Is there a battle or quest underway? What sort of jobs do they have?

If you are creating your own world, it is best to make it a normal world which has just that something a little bit different about it. This makes it more believable to the reader.

Draw up a map so you can see the layout of your fantasy world. This can help avoid the risk of making mistakes or contradicting yourself.

You might not need to use every single aspect of the information you have collated within your story. But it is useful to have the information at hand as and when you need it.

Science fiction

This is effectively a fantasy world set in the future. It offers an opportunity to consider what the Earth may be like several centuries ahead, or to consider life on other planets, and the possibilities presented by space travel.

Creating such a world requires you to take the world you know and add all kinds of amazing features. Try replacing cars with hover cars, or jet-propelled pads which allow people to travel instantly from place to place; or just simply ways of speeding up a walking pace.

What might wait down a black hole? What would it be like going through a black hole in space? The only limits such settings face, are those which are provided by your own imagination. As with any other setting, you need to really know it and let it live within your own imagination. Ask yourself all the same questions as detailed in fantasy worlds – who rules? What type of food? How do they move?

The opportunities are tremendous once you let your imagination run riot. Science fiction is enjoyed by all age ranges. Published books have included portraying cows and dinosaurs as astronauts encountering pirates and dust storms.

Your setting has to be believable. Don't try to change everything. Keep some things which are familiar. There may horses and goats in your story, but you can add in moverins and burins.

'If you are creating your own world, it is best to make it a normal world which has just that something a little bit different about it. This makes it more believable to the reader.'

Elements of science fiction, real worlds and fantasy worlds can be combined. Perhaps elves fly through space on aeroplanes, or magic provides power in an alien world.

Checklist

- Keep settings believeable.
- Don't try to change everything.
- Know your creation in detail.

Creating locations

'Travel magazines and brochures from travel agents can be very helpful in creating locations.'

Simply sitting down and creating a location from scratch is hard work. At that point, most people will struggle. Aids are necessary.

This is where your notebooks will come in very useful. Notebooks should be used to keep notes of any interesting, unusual or notable locations that you see. Take photographs or buy postcards. Look for unusual pictures in the newspapers. A very cold period in Norfolk resulted in a hedge being totally covered in icicles. A picture was given in the local newspaper and promptly cut and added to a notebook. Somewhere, sometime, that image can be reused in a future location.

Jot down names of places that catch your attention. Look at names on signposts or ways of directing people around a location. Country roads in Norfolk are often given the sign 'byway'. This could lead to anywhere and immediately makes the imagination of a writer run riot.

Travel magazines and brochures from travel agents can be very helpful in creating locations. Choose a picture and see if you can use it as the background for a story. Describe what you see and imagine that it has suddenly come alive. What happens next? Does the weather change? Does someone fall in the river? A plane crosses the mountains and crashes? A ship crewed by fauns lands on the beach?

Catalogues and magazines might give ideas for house or room interiors. Look in seed catalogues for pictures of flowers or gardens.

Try playing a location creation game. All you need are some appropriate lists and allot them numbers from one or more dice. The more tables of options available, the more detailed your location. Throw the dice and see what number is revealed. Write down the matching location.

For example:

Real settings

Terrain

1 Rolling hills

2 Rocky

3 Smooth

4 Steep gradient

5 Water

6 Desert

Buildings

1. Townscapes

2 Villages

3 Castles

4 Farms

5 Skyscrapers

6. Houses

Geographical features

1. Hills

2. Mountains

3. Lakes

4. Caves

5. Forests

6. Roads

Weather

1. Clouds

2. Sunshine

3. Rain

4. Wind

5. Storms

8. Snow

Time

1. Day

2. Night

3. Morning

4. Noon

5. Evening

Transport

1. Motor vehicles

2. Horses

3. Spacecraft

4. Boats

5. Aircraft

6. Afternoon	6. Trains.

So if you roll Terrain 1, Buildings 4, Geographical features 4, Weather 3, Time 4 and Transport 4 the result is a location which has rolling hills with caves and dotted with farms. It is noon and raining. Transport is by boat so there must have been some flooding.

Checklist

- Keep notebooks.
- Look out for names, places and interesting features.
- Write down details and references.

Description

When describing locations use small sections of description rather than several paragraphs or great chunks of words. A good way is to use a little bit of detail at a time. It could be passed on as a descriptive sentence or incorporated into a passage of dialogue.

For example:

The trees grew right up to the castle walls, making a thick, tangled forest. It was frightening.

Instead, you might write:

'I'm really, really frightened of going into that forest. The trees are so thick and the branches are so tangled. It feels like they are trying to capture me,' said Barbara.

'But I've heard there is a castle hidden in there. It would be fantastic to find it,' said James.

Summing Up

- Be accurate when dealing with real or historical settings.
- Make sure you know your locations.
- Use description carefully.
- Do not overpower your reader with detail.

Chapter Five

Developing a Plot

A good plot is absolutely crucial to any story. It is the plot that keeps the reader turning the pages and wanting to know what happens next. If the plot does not get their attention – then the book will be ignored. No one will read it.

Plotting

For every plot you need to work out:

- What is the story about?
- When does it take place?
- What is the problem?
- Who is involved?
- Who resolves the problem?
- How is the problem resolved?

Remember that the hero or heroine has to play a key part in finding and providing a solution to the problem. The solution should not be just provided by someone else.

As you plot out your story, you need to include elements of tension. The longer the story, the more tension-filled sections you will need. After each example of tension, there should be a slightly calmer period. Imagine it as being like a going up and down series of hills, which steadily get larger and larger, until the final climax is reached. Then as the characters make their way down from that final hill (or climax) all the loose ends are gathered up and tied together.

Plot lines can come in many different formats. Common themes are:

'A good plot is absolutely crucial to any story. It is the plot that keeps the reader turning the pages and wanting to know what happens next.'

Achievement

The central character has to achieve a desired aim. In the Angelina Ballerina books, the heroine is a little mouse who wants to be a ballet dancer.

Battles

The hero/heroine has to deal with a foe. This could be an unpleasant person, an awkward teacher, sibling rivalry, a newcomer.

Humour

Any situation that a child might encounter can be given a humorous overtone. The best example of this type of writing are the *Horrid Henry* stories.

Mistakes

Problems which have to be dealt with, for example pressing the wrong button and erasing material on a computer, forgetting to pass on a message, or putting the wrong ingredient in a spell.

Mysteries and puzzles

The hero or heroine has to solve the problem. It might be a major problem as in the *Roman Mysteries* by Caroline Lawrence, where children are captured by slave traders, or a simple loss of an object like a ring or a pet. This is a typical theme in fairy stories.

Quests

This is a popular theme in most genres. It could be a quest for a magic sword, or a treasure hunt that goes wrong. The Narnia stories are typical quests involving fantasy and adventure.

Revenge

The hero wants to get revenge on another character. It might be as part of a feud or argument that has gone wrong.

Tragedy

A difficult plot line as you have to ensure you do not upset children. If tragedy occurs – a car accident or a death – then the story must end on a positive note. Admittedly, there have been exceptions to this rule. The Lemony Snicket stories entitled *A Series of Unfortunate Events* involved everything that could possible go wrong, happening. It proved successful because the setting involved a slightly fantastical element, children could feel that it was a little remote from their own experiences, and there was always a touch of humour to lighten the tale.

Transformations

A classic element found in many fairy stories. The Ugly Duckling turns into a swan, Cinderella changes from a scruffy servant into a sparkling princess. A mysterious stranger might arrive and transform a situation as in *Mary Poppins* or *Nanny McPhee*.

Most good plot lines incorporate several of these elements. A heroine might want to win a horse riding competition, but has lost her way. Having found a magic sword, a hero is sent on a quest but to achieve success has to overcome a family feud. When combining in this way, take care not to make the plot line so complex that children cannot follow it.

Storylines should be exciting and interesting. There should be lots of cliffhangers, unexpected twists and surprises designed to keep the reader turning the pages until the very end of the story. While the age range of your potential reader should be borne in mind as you create the plot, do not make it your exclusive concern. Concentrate on creating the best plot line you can, as the plot may result in having a much wider audience than initially planned. Confident readers do tend to read around and choose books which are not necessarily designed for their age group. A six-year-old may well be able to read a book aimed at a nine or ten-year-old.

Checklist

* Work out your plot.
* Include plenty of tension.
* Make sure loose ends are gathered up.
* Read children's fiction and identify themes.
* Study published books and identify which type of plot is involved.
* Explore which combinations of plots are being used.

Plots and subplots

Apart from very simple stories designed for young children, books normally have at least one or two subplots underlying the main story. In Cinderella there is a main plot and a subplot:

Plot – Cinderella is unhappy because her stepmother has turned her into a servant.

Subplot – Her stepsisters are looking for ways to make her life even more unhappy.

Plot – The prince is looking for a bride, and invites all the girls in his country to a ball.

Subplot – The stepsisters and stepmother prevent Cinderella from attending.

Plot – Cinderella goes to the ball with the aid of her fairy godmother. She has a lovely time, and meets the prince. Has to flee from the ball, leaving her shoe behind.

Plot – The prince orders that every girl must try on the shoe so he can find the girl he loves.

Subplot – The stepsisters try to prevent Cinderella from trying on the shoe

Plot – Cinderella tries the shoe and it fits. She becomes the prince's bride.

Analysing stories like this, will help you learn how to link plots and subplots together. If you lay out your plot outline in a similar fashion it will reduce the chance of leaving any loose ends unfinished at the end of the story.

'Apart from very simple stories designed for young children, books normally have at least one or two subplots underlying the main story.'

Checklist

■ Having both a plot and subplot helps to move the story along.

■ It makes your story more complex and interesting.

Need2Know

Beginning, middle and end

The beginning of a new book is crucial. The first two or three paragraphs have to grab your reader's attention. By the end of the page, they should be so caught up in the story that they must turn the page to find out what happens next.

Starting with something unusual happening is always a good hook. It should be something different, something in the world changes – the church clock strikes 13; your character is informed that they are going away; there is an argument; trouble begins, or someone arrives who changes everything.

The middle of the story is where the characters face problems in achieving a desired end. They encounter problems and conflicts. Typical obstacles for the hero to overcome might be:

- Illness.

- Mistakes – letters are delivered to the wrong address, goes to an event on the wrong day.

- Problems – school difficulties, a pet goes missing.

- A device of some kind fails – a car breaks down, a computer crashes.

- Death.

- Disaster – an earthquake, a fire.

The final showdown or climax is where all the pieces of the plot pull together. Do not cheat your reader by suddenly having a very easy ending such as 'It was all a dream'.

Checklist

- Get your reader's attention at the beginning.

- Ensure your story has a beginning, middle and an end.

- Make sure the middle of a story has tension, conflicts or obstacles the hero/ heroine has to overcome.

Plot outlines

Practise creating plot outlines. These outlines should be no more than one page long. Take a simple idea, such as a school bag, and ask yourself questions. What if there was something hidden inside the bag? What might it be? Could it be a special tool, a book which leads into other worlds, a museum artefact, a tiny alien? What if the bag suddenly started getting heavier and heavier, and on opening it you find that the contents are multiplying rapidly, making copies upon copies of books? Use these questions to develop a plot outline.

It may help to make up a story map. Create a map of your story world and indicate on it where the different stages of the action take place. This can help identify information you need to provide such as how the characters travel from place to place, or highlight unexpected problems that they may have to overcome. Do they take the quickest route via a mountain range even though it is in the middle of winter, or do they try a longer route by river?

It is very important to remember to stay within your allotted number of words. Do not let the story run away from you – you will have to do a lot of editing afterwards. Give yourself an approximate number of words per chapter, for example a 10,000 word book might have 1,000 words per chapter. This can only be an estimate – some chapters may have to be longer than others.

Summing Up

- Stories must have a beginning, middle and an end.
- Stories need a mix of plot and subplot.
- Include plenty of tension.
- Make sure your ending gathers up all the loose ends.

Chapter Six

Writing Technique

Practice is the most important way you can improve your writing technique. You must look at all aspects of writing from plotting, to introductions, endings and viewpoints.

Writing perspective

Books can be written from different perspectives. You need to work out which viewpoint suits your style of writing, as well as what suits the storyline.

The most common viewpoint is that of the narrator. This is a traditional story-telling technique. The narrator stands slightly apart from the story, and recounts what is happening. Sometimes this is also referred to as writing from a third person viewpoint. Characters are referred to by name, or using words such as 'he', 'she', 'they' or 'it'.

First person narration is quite hard to do. It tells the story from one person's viewpoint, and it is this character with whom the reader is going to identify. It is essential to have a strong, well-drawn character telling the story, and as a writer you really need to know that character well. A typical sentence would be 'I lived in the village of Wood End'. The word 'I' is used a lot throughout the story and you have to take care not to make it appear monotonous. It can be a limiting format as it does not offer opportunities to see the story from the viewpoint of other characters.

If writing in the first person, make sure that the tone of the story will appeal to your readers. A whining teenager will not appeal, whereas a boy facing major problems and dealing with those problems by showing increasing courage or humour will be much more acceptable. The reader has to be kept interested and encouraged to continue reading, turning the pages until the very end of the book is reached.

'First person narration is quite hard to do.'

Sometimes books are told from multiple viewpoints. This is even harder than writing first person narrative. Each chapter is told from the viewpoint of a different person, usually two characters each taking an alternate chapter. Multiple viewpoints of this kind are not easy for children to read, and it can become very confusing.

The viewpoint from which you write can change the focus of the story. Each character in a story looks at the plot in a different way.

To decide which type of writing suits you and the storyline, experiment with stories written for the different viewpoints. Create stories using each viewpoint. A good exercise is to take a minor character from an existing story and try writing the story from their viewpoint. This will immediately alter the storyline, because that character will see things differently to the main character. This demonstrates just how carefully you need to choose your writing style.

Having tried out the different types of writing, ask yourself which style you feel happiest writing and which works best for the story. Remember that some storylines may work better in first person, while others will be better in third person or from a multiple viewpoint. Above all, remember that, as a writer, your task is to draw the reader into the story. The writer has to become invisible no matter what viewpoint is used.

Checklist

- Choose your viewpoint: first person, narrator/third person, multiple viewpoint.

- Decide what suits you and your story.

- Which style do you feel happiest using?

Tenses

Language uses difference tenses – past, present, future. It is important to use the right tense to reflect an action.

Consider too the age range for which you are writing. If sentences are too complex in their construction, you will lose your reader. They may not understand the differences in tenses.

The present tense is the usual means by which books for the very young are written. 'We are at the zoo. The monkeys are playing'. It tells of events that are happening at that moment.

As children get older, the past tense becomes more common. 'He went to the shops. His dog followed him'. The past tense refers to events that have taken place.

The future tense refers to events that may take place at some point. 'We will go to the zoo on Monday'. Most children over the age of 5 can understand differences between present and future, and are beginning to understand the concept of the past.

Language

The language used in a book should be challenging for a child, yet within their capabilities. As children grow older, they learn more words and can cope with more complex grammatical structures.

Explore the techniques of writing for different ages. Look at the words used in books for different age groups – preschool, 5-7, 8-10, 10+ and teenagers. Then try and write your own short stories or simply a letter aimed at each of the age groups. Use the same topic as this will identify the changes needed in the amount of information and the words used.

Getting the words right will be particularly important when writing educational books designed for literacy teaching. Having been provided with a list of words that must be included, you will need to make sure that all those words are used in the required way.

Always try and put yourself into the mind of a child. This can make it easier to write for them as you begin to appreciate how they see the world.

Analyse stories

Analysing published stories is a good way of improving your own writing. Look at the way the author has created the plot line, the type of characters that have been used, how they have used dialogue to move the story along or to give information.

'The present tense is the usual means by which books for the very young are written.'

Identify the different viewpoints that have been used. Do you feel that the author was right to use that particular viewpoint? Could it have been done better from a different viewpoint?

Read the book aloud. Listen to any use of rhythm. Consider too how the author has created tension within the plot. What words are used to create an atmosphere or a feeling that something is about to happen?

Having analysed some stories, look back at your own writing and see how you could incorporate what you have learned in a story.

Checklist

- Analyse stories and information books to see what words have been used, how the plot line is maintained, and characterisation.

- Identify how you are using words and information.

- Read books aloud and listen for any rhythm.

Wordage

Take a children's book and count up how many words it has. If there are lots of pages, count up the words on an average page and multiply it by the number of pages overall. This will give you an estimated size.

Then write a page from the book using a different viewpoint. You could use first person if it has been written in a general style. Try and keep to the same number of words on the page. It is harder than it looks as you have to change so much.

Study the words that have been used by the author. What are the most difficult words and the most common words used? Ask yourself how this compares to your own writing.

Rupert annuals can be a very useful aid when improving your own writing. Each story within a Rupert annual has two formats: one involves rhyming couplets, while the other is a much longer narration. It shows how the same story can be read from different viewpoints, and different writing styles.

Keeping to the correct number of words is essential for any writer. You cannot just simply write and think that every word is going to be published. Extensive editing requirements can be minimised by practising good writing techniques. Practise writing to a set wordage. This is a technique that can be learned.

A good way to practise is to take a story from a newspaper. Count the number of words. Then edit it down to a quarter of the length, without losing any information or the flow of the story.

Set yourself a specific number of words for a story. It could be 500 or 1,000 words. Then write your story to match that exact number of words. This helps you to focus on exactly what you need to put in to the story. Make sure you cover all sections of the storyline. If you find yourself struggling at the end, trying to cram all the information in that is needed to end the story, then it shows you need to look more closely at the earlier sections. What could be cut down?

Then, take the story that you have written and rewrite it. This time aim to reduce the number of words by half. Exercises of this type will ensure that you focus on your use of words, and learn to use only those words that are absolutely essential.

Checklist

- Keep to the exact number of words required.
- Do not go over or under that limit.
- Use only words which are essential to the story.

Dialogue

Dialogue is essential to break up the flow of the story, and can make a considerable contribution to developing storylines. It can be used to increase the reader's knowledge of a character, or to move the plot onwards. Dialogue can also be used to provide explanations.

But, when you write dialogue it is important to make very clear just who is speaking. If you write too many he saids or she saids, or simply have lines of speech, you can lose your reader. It is easy to lose track of who said something or where the conversation is going.

With older readers, you can vary the language and use other options: he thought, he grinned, he laughed. Or you can show a reaction as the character fulfils an act.

John smiled as he opened the door. 'Hello'.

One character might say, 'Let's go and find out.' There's no need to write an answer in dialogue. You just carry on with the story indicating what happens next.

Dialogue is a useful method of providing information about characters or events. Instead of writing that a character loves ice cream, you could let it be known through dialogue. On a hot day, she invites someone to have an ice cream – 'Let's go and get some ice cream from the shop. It's really yummy, smooth and cooling on a day like this.'

Ask yourself what the dialogue says about a character. Someone using lots of long words might be trying to show themselves to be more educated than they are, or are trying to impress another character.

Do not allow one character to talk for too long. Long speeches can lose the reader's attention. Use interruptions to break up the flow of the character's words. Aim for about three sentences before letting someone else speak.

Do not use complicated tenses or complicated sentences with lots of different punctuation. Books targeting young children should have simple dialogue. Avoid stating the obvious. If a picture shows Jenny going to the cinema, there is no need to say, 'Can we go to the cinema?'

To improve your use of dialogue, listen carefully to conversations on buses, in cafés, or on TV. Note how people speak. Identify characteristic phrases and words that are used. Some people frequently end sentences with the words 'I know' or 'I do'. Make a note of them, and how they can be used to identify someone when writing dialogue.

Need2Know

In normal speech, we tend to use lots of digressions; repeating words and phrases as well as using 'er'. Ignore these, and don't include in your dialogue unless it is absolutely necessary as a way of portraying a character.

Dialect is best avoided, especially for young children as it can confuse. Similarly avoid slang or current idioms and phrases. These may not be in use by the time the book is published. It can make your book seem dated in a very short time. A further problem is that slang may not be understood by overseas readers – and this could ruin your chances of being involved in co-editions; or even reduce your chances of having the book accepted for publication.

Checklist

- Make it clear who is speaking.
- Use dialogue to provide information about a character or a place.
- Avoid dialect.
- Avoid stating obvious facts.

Cultural awareness

As you write, it is important to bear in mind differences between cultures. If your book is to be successful and sell lots of copies, universal appeal is essential. This is particularly important with regard to picture books where co-editions are extremely important.

The storyline should be understandable in most countries of the world, just as much in the US, Australia or Germany as in the UK. Avoid subjects and references which might be confusing. A black cat brings luck if crossing your path in the UK – in Italy it is the exact opposite, as the same action brings bad luck.

Remember that there are linguistic differences even among English speaking countries. American English is similar but not identical to the English spoken in England. Differences do exist.

For example, in the UK, letters are delivered by a postman or postwoman. In the US, a mailman delivers letters. In the UK, the letters are pushed through a letterbox. In the US, the letters are left in a mailbox at the gate.

'Dialect is best avoided, especially for young children as it can confuse.'

People walk on the pavement in the UK. In the US, people walk on the sidewalk. Children play in the back garden in the UK, while across the Atlantic they play in the backyard.

Checklist

- Consider cultural differences.

- Watch out for linguistic differences.

- You can get computer programs which will deal with linguistic differences between English and American English.

Summing Up

- Identify your viewpoint.
- Analyse stories to improve your writing.
- Keep to the required length.

Chapter Seven

How to Edit and be Ruthless About Your Work

Having written your book, you now have to edit it. This is possibly the hardest task of any writer. It is very hard to admit that you may need to change words and remove sections from the story. You must learn to be ruthless.

Editing is very important. After completing the first draft of the book, you need to read it several times with a very critical eye. If you cannot do this yourself, get someone else to do it for you. It has to be done carefully and thoroughly so that no mistake is missed.

Begin by looking for all spelling mistakes, missed words, punctuation and grammatical errors. A good spellchecking facility on your computer will prove invaluable at this point! But do not rely solely on a computer spellcheck. It can pass a word or date as being correct, but you might have made a mistake in the way a word is used, or in numbers. I have written books in which everything seemed fine, until I physically checked every word only to discover that I had mistakenly typed 1936 for 1836. Numerical errors in a science or mathematics book could be catastrophic and cause major problems. Ultimately, if a publisher starts getting complaints about accuracy, then they are less likely to use you again in the future.

Look too at the storyline. All loose ends should be carefully tied up in the final chapter. Nothing should be left outstanding – unless you are planning a sequel to answer those questions.

Having done all this, it is time to look at what you have actually written. Are there any sections that are too descriptive? Could they be cut back? Long passages of description should be avoided. It is better to remove them, or split them into smaller sections to be used within the storyline or dialogue. Are there any sections that ought to be expanded to create a better plot line? Remove any weak points in the story. Replace these with an improved section.

Ask yourself:

- Does the story follow a logical sequence?
- Are all the subplots resolved when the book comes to an end?
- Can the reader tell the characters apart when they are speaking?
- Could the dialogue be shorter?
- Are there any unnecessary or repetitive words?

Identify any repetitive sections. Have you repeated information in more than one chapter? If so, such repetitions should be removed.

Every word in the book should be essential to the story. There should be no overwriting, such as too much description. Always ask yourself, should these words or phrases be included? Are they essential to the story? Make each word count.

'Every word in the book should be essential to the story. There should be no overwriting, such as too much description.'

Checklist

- Have you done a spellcheck and grammar check?
- Are there any loose ends?
- Have all the subplots and main plot been brought to a satisfactory end?
- Is there any repetition?

Beginnings and endings

Read through the opening paragraphs of your first chapter. Could those paragraphs be improved? The reader's interest must be grabbed within the first two or three paragraphs – otherwise you may have lost them for good. You have got to convince the reader to carry on reading, for example by providing hints of unexpected happenings, mysteries or something strange happening, or problems developing. Starting a book with the words, 'It was midnight and the clock struck 12' doesn't stand out. Starting the story with the words, 'It was midnight when the clock struck 13', is a very different matter. The reader immediately wonders, why 13? What's the problem? What's happened?

Look at the endings of chapters – do they lead nicely onto the next instalment? End some chapters on cliffhangers – material designed to keep the reader compulsively turning the pages to find out what happens next. Keep the pace and tension moving.

Make sure that the final number of words actually matches the publisher's requirements. If a publisher is looking for a 10,000 word story – then that is exactly what they want. They do not want 20,000 words or even 15,000 words.

As you edit your manuscript, consider where it is potentially going to be used. If you are aiming for Internet publishing or an e-book, sentences and paragraphs need to be much shorter than in conventional publishing. This reflects the type of screen such as an iPad upon which the manuscript may be read.

Criticism

If a book is designed for reading aloud then read it aloud. Check that it has the right rhythm and sounds good when someone is listening to it. Reading aloud can help ensure that punctuation is correct. It is very easy to write long sentences and forget such minor things as commas and full stops. Reading aloud suddenly makes you realise that something is missing. It can show too where action is developing or tension is rising.

Do not rely on your own instincts. As the author, it can be hard to judge and criticise your own work. Ask for the opinions of other people, especially children. They can be very harsh critics.

Whatever the book, you do need to get other people's opinions and criticisms. Ask children for their reaction. Avoid asking your own children – they will be too polite, as they do not want to upset you. Try contacting local libraries and ask if you can read your story at a children's storytime, or in a local school. There may be a Brownie pack or preschool that can help.

It is possible to search for Internet partners to criticise each other's work. This works by sending a chapter to your partner to read. They criticise it and send you their work for criticism.

Find out if there is a writers' group in your area. These can be very helpful and a good way of getting criticism. They can also provide encouragement when it feels you are not getting anywhere with a writing project, sometimes providing much needed inspiration. Your local library will know of any such groups.

Checklist

- Ask for criticism.
- Seek help and comments from playgroups, Brownie packs, libraries, schools.
- Do not rely on your own instincts.

'Editing is a key part of the publication process, leading to a finished story which can be approved by both publisher and author.'

Publishers and editing

Even after you have edited your manuscript and submitted it to a publisher or agent, be prepared to undertake more revisions. Editing is a key part of the publication process, leading to a finished story which can be approved by both publisher and author.

The publishers will give the manuscript to a specialist reader who checks it for problems and inconsistencies. A reader seeks to identify items like a dog which changes breed in the middle of the story, or for loose ends of the plot that have not been tied up. They consider whether there is too much description or too much dialogue, whether it adds anything to a story or should be removed.

The editor provides lots of queries, which need to be answered quickly. They may ask you to rewrite a chapter, then having looked at the manuscript again, ask for more rewriting. This process can go on for some time. Be prepared to cut, reduce wordage and to edit as required. It may be the only way that the story can be published and you will need to consider carefully all that they say.

If you really feel that a particular scene is essential and should be retained, you need to explain why. It may be that it is a key scene that helps explain why an event happens, or a character takes a particular action much further on in the book. If you can convince your editor, then you may be allowed to keep the scene.

The aim is always to make sure that the book is suitable for publication.

When the editing process is finally complete, you will be sent the page proofs. These will need to be read through and checked. Sometimes printers accidentally move sections or put in a heading where there should not be a heading.

For example, in my book *Travelling with Kids* I gave details of a counting game. When I checked the page proofs I was puzzled to see a new game that I had not written called How Many Logos? When I looked at what I had originally written, I discovered that the printers had accidentally split the counting game and turned a question into a heading. This meant that the page proof no longer made any sense. My editor quite rightly had flagged it up asking for changes.

Editing is a long, painstaking process. It is important to be meticulous and check thoroughly. This is even more important when writing non-fiction. Mistakes can be made and the editing process is where they can be corrected.

'Editing is a long, painstaking process. It is important to be meticulous and check thoroughly.'

Summing Up

- Be ruthless when editing. Remember that material taken out could be used elsewhere in other stories. Store it in a separate file for future use.

- Seek critical advice.

- Make every word count.

- Be meticulous in checking and editing.

Chapter Eight

Illustration, Picture and Games Books

The market for illustrated and picture books is a very distinct sector. As a writer, concentrate on the text – leave the illustrations to an artist. Unless you are already a skilled artist, there is no point attempting to illustrate your own work.

Most authors will only be involved in writing a story. Unless you are a trained artist, sending illustrations to accompany a story will be a waste of time. Publishers prefer to use trained artists to undertake book illustrations. You may be asked for your opinion and will see the illustrations before they go to print, but the final decision will remain with the publisher.

The most common types of illustrated books are:

Board books

Board books for babies and toddlers are the simplest form of children's writing. They usually involve nursery rhymes, counting rhymes, or some simple words and pictures. For first-time writers there are very few opportunities in this field. The books require illustration skills rather than writing, and will normally be prepared using established writers and illustrators known to the publishing company.

Picture books

Books for younger children always involve a mix of pictures and words. Young children need to be able to look at pictures in order to help them understand the story. Repetition of words is very important, as this helps children to learn to read and understand the story. As the stories are designed to be read aloud, the rhythm of words should be borne in mind, together with the use of repetitive phrases and words. Plot lines are simple, easy to understand and catch the attention. Children can follow the theme of the story simply by looking at the pictures. The pictures are always large and colourful. The quality of the illustrations is always extremely important.

Given that these stories are often read at bedtime, there should be nothing to cause nightmares. The last thing you want is to have parents complaining!

Picture books are aimed at children between 2 and 6 years old, and generally have around 32 pages with lots of colour illustrations. No story is ever more than 1,000 words long, and usually much shorter, at around 400 words. Stories for picture books need a clear start, middle and end. Study existing books carefully to see what is being written. Avoid conventional themes like starting school or the arrival of a new baby – these have been done exhaustively. Publishers will not be interested. Look for new slants and new ideas. Good books to study in this sector include Michael Rosen's *We're Going on a Bear Hunt*; *Kipper*, by Mick Inkpen; *Maisy* by Lucy Cousins and *Elmer* by David McKee

'Stories for picture books need a clear start, middle and end.'

The Maisy books are particularly useful as study material as they show how the character has developed and changed, and new series developed. Apart from stories about Maisy, there is a series focusing on Maisy First Experiences . . . which includes *Maisy Goes to Nursery*, *Maisy Goes to the Museum*, *Maisy Goes to the Library*. In *Maisy Goes to the City* we see how Maisy and Charley visit Dotty who has moved to the city. Dotty shows them all the sights including big buildings and the Underground. The accompanying artwork is designed to convey the experience of going to an unfamiliar big city.

When writing this type of book, you have to be very economical with your words. Every word has got to count and move the plot along. Pages can contain as few as 14 words. The text has to be spread equally across all 12 double pages. The text can be laid out in several different ways:

- At the top or bottom of the page.
- In empty space left by the illustrator.
- In two or three blocks of words.

- On one page with the illustration on the opposite page.

It is essential that a writer of picture books is able to think in terms of pictures. You have to visualise your book in pictures, and write it accordingly. The words and pictures together have to move the story onwards.

The writer can provide a note about what the characters look like, and the settings in which the characters appear when sending the finished story down to the publisher. These guidelines will be borne in mind by the illustrator commissioned to create the pictures.

These books are expensive to publish, and usually require international co-editions. The costs have to be minimised in order to ensure that the final purchase price is acceptable to the consumer. Prices have to be kept low. The larger the print run, the lower the final price of the book. Having overseas co-editions means that the price can be kept down.

Be warned that it can take a long time to produce a picture book. The process of publication is lengthy. After signing a contract to publish a story, time has to be allowed for editorial checks, making amendments, organising an illustrator, commissioning illustrations and cover, waiting for illustrations to be made, agreeing the illustrations, creating proofs, contacting publishers regarding possible co-editions overseas, printing the pages, checking the page proofs, organising distribution and marketing. At the end of that process, the book is finally printed and ready for sale in the shops.

Checklist

- Practise writing to pictures.
- Keep the text short and simple.
- Make every word count.

Novelty books

These include pop-up books and mixed media books (books which include materials to touch). Books of this kind are particularly suitable for young children, but are sometimes used in non-fiction for older children. They can involve pulling tabs, pop-up scenes, turning wheels, lift the flap, slide along the

'It is essential that a writer of picture books is able to think in terms of pictures. You have to visualise your book in pictures, and write it accordingly. The words and pictures together have to move the story onwards.'

slot. Opportunities for first-time authors are virtually non-existent. Such books cost a lot to produce. Publishers prefer to commission such books from authors they already know and whose work can be guaranteed to be at the required standard.

Younger fiction

These are stories which are designed for children learning to read, and becoming confident readers. Around 1,000 to 1,500 words long, they will often include some black and white illustrations.

Plot lines can be more varied and cover a variety of genres including historical, fantasy, magic, real life, animals and nature. Real-life stories should concentrate on issues which a child will understand such as the type of experiences they encounter, and emotions like joy, misery, jealousy, anxiety and fear. Ask yourself, what would make a child anxious or fearful? What storylines could be used to bring out these emotions? There should always be a way out of the problem, and a happy ending.

As children get older, the number of pictures contained within a story become less. There may be maps, decorative edgings to the start of chapters, and sometimes, small line drawings. In the *Chrestomanci* books by Diana Wynne Jones, there are small black and white line drawings at the start of each chapter. These show one scene or object or character from that particular chapter. Such drawings are very much an adjunct to the text. The words have become the most important element.

Puzzle books

These can include highly decorative images which might involve only a short paragraph of informative text. Typical of this type of book is *Pirates,* by Anna Nilsen; and the *Usborne Puzzle World* series.

Non-fiction illustrated books

These are common for all age groups and across all curriculum subjects. Again, the pictures will be provided by artists and photographers and is a very different market to that of the writer. There are some people who can both write and illustrate – but they have very specialist skills and knowledge. Unless you possess art skills as well as writing skills, concentrate on just one form of work.

The market for non-fiction illustrated books is extensive. They help to bring subjects alive for children, providing visual information to back up the written word.

Graphic books

This sector is an expanding market. The growth of Japanese manga-style stories has helped to revitalise it.

Manga is very different to traditional comic books and needs careful study from potential writers. Manga books have generally been imported from Japan, where they are a major industry. Japanese-style manga books are read in reverse order to conventional books – from the back to the front. A growing number of manga books are now being published by UK and US publishers and these are read from front to back. Fantasy and horror, usually with a touch of romance, tend to dominate manga books. The style of illustrations is distinctive in terms of clothes, facial features and the type of characters being used.

Graphic books are more akin to traditional comic books, with the whole story being told in a strip format. Adults as well as children read graphic novels. In some countries like France and Belgium, graphic books are big business. Good examples include the stories of Asterix and Tintin. Some writers have specialised in this format. To be successful, a writer must also be a good illustrator. Marcia Williams has compiled many popular graphic books which tell classic stories such as the tales of Shakespeare, King Arthur, Robin Hood, Charles Dickens, Ancient Egyptian myths, The Iliad and the Odyssey. Her skill lies in providing amusing drawings which link clearly into the accompanying text.

'Graphic books are more akin to traditional comic books, with the whole story being told in a strip format.'

Graphic novels have to be very tightly scripted. It is important for the writer to be able to imagine the story as a series of boxes – a pictorial story board. Written information is mainly provided in speech bubbles or in small scrolls of narration above or below the picture. The same rules of plotting and characterisation to be found in any story are always followed in graphic books.

Checklist

- Manga books are different to comic books.
- Study the characters.
- Study the way words and pictures combine to tell the story.

Games books

This is quite a big market, particularly among books for boys. The high level of reader participation which is involved in games books, together with the adventurous style means that that this style of books appeals to boys, even reluctant readers. Part story, part game these books require readers to not only read the story, but to make decisions and decide where the story will go.

The most well-known series of games books are the *Fighting Fantasy* series written by Ian Livingstone and Steve Jackson. Many of these books were originally published a decade ago, but are now being republished to meet the interest of a new audience. New books in the series are being created. The stories are very complex.

A typical storyline is that of the *Forest of Doom* by Ian Livingstone. The reader is asked to go on a journey into Darkwood Forest to find the missing pieces of the legendary Hammer of Stonebridge. But the journey is not without its risks – along the way the reader can encounter all kinds of problems and hazards. To succeed, the reader has to find the master magician Yaztromo and restore the Hammer before the trolls destroy Stonebridge forever.

These books are not straightforward books. After an introduction to the plot, the reader has to decide what is going to happen next. A pencil and eraser are essential to keep track of what is happening. The reader has decide which route to take, which creatures to fight and which dangers to risk. Rolling a dice will sometimes indicate where the reader has to go, it could be anywhere –

backwards or forwards. Each section has a number and the reader has to go to the allotted number. For example, faced with a choice between turning east or west in a tunnel, the reader has to choose – then move to the appropriate number. The reader's progress within the story can be made more complex by the need to obtain stamina points and provisions along the way.

Ultimately, the reader may be fortunate and find their way successfully to the end of the story – or then again, the reader can be killed and have to start all over again, making new choices. It can be an extremely irritating and frustrating process, but one which definitely keeps the reader turning the page!

Writing these books is definitely complex. Keeping control of the storyline and all the variations requires a lot of concentration on the part of the writer. Each book provides an introduction to the story, characters and problem before play commences. It is a challenging format but one which can be very successful and develop a long-term following among potential readers.

There have been other series of this kind. *Appointment With F.E.A.R* is a science fiction version of *Fighting Fantasy*, and there have been detective series where the reader is required to solve a mystery. *The Lone Wolf* fantasy game books provided quest type challenges to solve. *Choose Your Way* is a series encouraging readers to find their way through unknown places like tropical forests or fairgrounds, and deal with all the problems they meet on the way. Some books focus on a historical battle and encourage the reader to take on the role of a general – can they make the right decisions based on clues and intelligence? The outcome of the battle may not be quite as they expect.

Whatever style of illustrated books you want to write, it is important to study what is already being published. See what is being reviewed on websites, or being sold in book clubs. Look at the books carefully and work out what makes them so successful. Ask yourself if there are any words that should not have been there? How do the illustrations link into the story? Does the text balance on each page? Do the pictures tell the story?

Summing Up

- Choose your preferred style of illustrated book.
- Look closely at how pictures and text combine to tell the story.
- Make the text balance within each set of pictures.

Chapter Nine

Writing Non-Fiction

Demand for non-fiction children's books is quite wide ranging, covering all kinds of material such as historical books, information, encyclopaedias, part-works, text books, nature and the environment.

The demands of the national curriculum must be borne in mind by any prospective writer of non-fiction books. Publishers will automatically be looking to gain sales in schools as a key part of their sales strategy – and schools are only interested if the material is linked into the national curriculum.

The national curriculum

The national curriculum has been laid down by successive governments for use by state schools in both the primary and secondary sectors. Each part of the curriculum is broken up into Key Stages.

Foundation or preschool	3-5 year-olds
Key Stage 1	5-7 year-olds
Key Stage 2	7-11 year-olds
Key Stage 3	11-13 year-olds
Key Stage 4	13-16 year-olds

Independent schools do not have to follow the demands of the national curriculum, but in practice teaching programmes tend to be linked to it. All published materials for the school market have to match the requirements of the national curriculum. Specific details of the national curriculum programme of study can be found on the official website http://curriculum.qcda.gov.uk. It also gives attainment targets for the appropriate Key Stages.

'Demand for non-fiction children's books is quite wide-ranging, covering all kinds of material such as historical books, information, encyclopaedias, part-works, text books, nature and the environment.'

The national curriculum is constantly changing, with new emphasisis being placed on different topics or new subjects being introduced. The arrival of the Olympics in 2012 meant that large amounts of teaching materials and non-fiction books were produced about the Olympics and topics arising from it. Would-be writers should keep careful watch on developments within the national curriculum. Changes mean that new learning materials have to be produced – and this provides an opportunity for writers to create suitable materials.

Alternative curriculums may sometimes be used. There is an international curriculum that some primary schools use which is designed to give a wider, international viewpoint. The International Baccalaureate is proving popular with some secondary schools, and independent schools unhappy with the GCSE/A level system.

All non-fiction material has to be authoritative. It has to provide something more than is available in existing books. Many educational books are written purely for use in schools – they are teaching aids. Topics can include all subjects covered within the curriculum including religious education, plays, poetry, history, geography, science, art and craft, mathematics. There are also workbooks for teachers which have to be produced.

Checklist

- Know the requirements of the national curriculum for your subject.
- Watch for amendments and changes being made.
- Identify any book opportunities that have been created.

Opportunities for good information books are present – it is just a matter of identifying them. Books like *Murderous Maths* and *Horrid Histories* have encouraged children to get interested in subjects beyond the requirements of the curriculum. Yet, at the same time, these books have linked into the curriculum and provided useful extra information.

Presentation is extremely important for children's non-fiction. Children have a short attention span and will not be attracted by long pages of words. The material has to be broken up into lots of sub sections, with individual headings and pictures. There should be plenty of boxes and side bars, rather than pages and pages of solid text. This type of layout encourages children to learn how to skim text so as to find out what they want.

Explore different ways of presenting information such as games, quizzes, activities and narratives.

A non-fiction book can be written in a reported style, or in a 'fictional' style telling a story around a fact. A book on Shakespeare might tell his story from his own viewpoint as he embarks on a career in the theatre. Other examples might be the tale of a refugee in World War Two, a nurse with Florence Nightingale in the Crimean War or a maid of honour serving Elizabeth I. Such books would tend to include a separate chapter giving background historical information.

Most non-fiction books form part of a series and follow a strict layout and have strict editorial requirements. A series of books on local history for children might request a short historical account for each period, followed by a semi-fictional account of a person within that period. For example:

- Romans and Saxons.

- Vikings and Norman conquest

- Medieval

- Tudors and Stuarts.

- Seventeenth/eighteenth centuries.

- Victorians to modern day.

Each of those sections would include a short story about a historical person in that period. A typical example might be:

'Hi, my name is Thomas. My father was a butcher in Ipswich. We lived over the shop. It was very noisy and busy. The animals were killed outside. I helped cut the meat and sell it in the shop. I thought I was going to be a butcher myself, but my father sent me to school. I did well and went to Cambridge University. I became a priest because this offered a good career. I was appointed to the royal court.

'Explore different ways of presenting information such as games, quizzes, activities and narratives.'

'When Henry VIII became king, I was one of his most trusted advisors. I helped him administer the country dealing with day-to-day matters, and helped make decisions on relationships with foreign countries. I became his Chancellor. The Pope made me a Cardinal, a prince of the Roman Catholic Church. I became very rich and powerful. I built a school in Ipswich and planned to make it into a university.

'All went well until the 'King's Great Matter' became important. Henry and his wife Catherine of Aragon had no sons, only a daughter called Mary. Henry wanted a divorce so he could marry Anne Boleyn – a much younger woman. The Church would not allow it. There were many arguments. Henry was very angry. I had failed him. He took away my job as Chancellor and arrested me. Henry said I was a traitor because I supported the Pope'.

> 'Proposals should be submitted to publishers with a covering letter, an outline of the proposed book and a sample chapter.'

Approaching publishers

When approaching publishers with an idea for a non-fiction book it is important to show how your proposed book will fit into the national curriculum. You will need to demonstrate expertise in your chosen subject and be enthusiastic about it. Teaching experience can be very useful.

Proposals should be submitted to publishers with a covering letter, an outline of the proposed book and a sample chapter. The covering letter should highlight your expertise and knowledge, target audience, as well as explaining what makes your book different from any other on the market.

Non-fiction books may result from the work of individual writers or from publishers and book packagers spotting a gap in the market. Sometimes publishers will approach a book packager to create a series. The packager will find the writers, illustrators and editors; usually paying a flat fee for the work rather than a royalty basis.

Indexes

You may be required to write an index for a non-fiction book. The best way to approach this task is to read through the book, listing down all the important points and subjects in alphabetical order. Most computer word processing facilities will be able to create alphabetical lists from your material.

When the page proofs come back, you will need to go through page by page noting down on which pages each word appears, for example:

Henry VIII – Pages 8, 10, 15, 20, 45.

Always double and treble check to make sure that your page numbers are correct.

Non-fiction magazines

This is a difficult but not impossible market to enter. Magazines have their own team of staff writers or known contributors who write all, or most of the material.

The first thing to do is to research your market. Look on the shelves at the newsagents to see what non-fiction magazines are being published. Identify the type of features and material that is being used in them. When you have found some magazines that are of interest to you, contact the publishers.

Ask if they use freelance submissions. Do not send anything without asking first. Provide ideas, giving a synopsis of what you are prepared to write and be prepared to provide a sample of your work if required. Always indicate your particular skills and expertise, showing why you are the ideal person to write this feature.

Timing is very important. Weekly magazines use more material than a monthly one, and have shorter deadlines. A monthly magazine is usually working two or three months ahead. Special issues like Christmas are generally commissioned in May/June and have been completed and are ready to be published by the autumn.

The other thing that is essential to bear in mind is that magazine editors want material that meets specific requirement. The feature should require little or no editing, meet the exact wordage and be on time. If the editor says the feature should be 800 words, then that is exactly what should be provided – not 850, 600 or 1,000. Magazines do not have time for lengthy editing, or asking for rewrites. If they commission material and it is unsuitable or late, they will simply not use you again.

Non-fiction magazine work can be good way of honing your writing skills, and getting your name known. Having work published in appropriate magazines, it shows you can write and meet deadlines. This can make it easier to move into the non-fiction book publishing sector because you will have achieved some experience.

'Non-fiction magazine work can be good way of honing your writing skills, and getting your name known.'

Summing Up

- Research your market.
- Know the requirements of the national curriculum.
- Be authoritative.
- Consider how you are presenting the material.

Chapter Ten

Finding an Audience

All stories need an audience. They are meant for sharing. What you have to do is decide what type of audience you are seeking. If you are happy just sharing your stories with family, friends and writers' groups, your task is much easier. Print off a few copies of your stories and pass them around.

But, if you are aiming to become a published author, it is a very different matter. You will need to be persistent and be prepared to accept that you will receive rejections. No author is published immediately. Even J K Rowling's book *Harry Potter and the Philosopher's Stone*, was turned down by several publishers, as was Beatrix Potter's *The Tale of Peter Rabbit* and Richard Adams' book *Watership Down*.

Publishing companies receive hundreds of manuscripts each day. Some will be immediately rejected on the basis of poor presentation, handwritten, or simply unsuitable for their list. Sending a children's book to a publisher who does not publish children's books is a waste of time.

Having carried out the initial cull of new manuscripts, editors put the scripts in order of priority.

Scripts submitted by agents are their first priority. Editors know that the agents will not be sending them useless stories, and that the stories have already undergone initial editing.

Next come manuscripts submitted by people they know or have been recommended by people they know. This includes authors already on their list.

At the bottom of the pile are all the other manuscripts. Often this section of the pile is called the 'slush pile'. There may be gems held within it, but it will take time for them to emerge and may depend entirely on who is doing the reading and whether the story appeals to them.

To find a publisher or agent, the best advice is to use the *Children's Writers' & Artists' Yearbook* published by Bloomsbury. This publication contains lists of all the publishers and indicates what type of book they publish. There is also a lot of very useful advice from published writers. You will need to study the Yearbook carefully, identifying which publishers to approach – and how to do so.

Presentation

The correct presentation is extremely important. No one accepts handwritten manuscripts. All material should be typed.

It is very easy to lose pages, so number them. Use double spacing on all the pages. This makes it easier to read.

Always include a covering letter stating what you are sending, a brief synopsis and indicate if you have had work published, and if so, where.

If you are approaching an educational or non-fiction publisher, check exactly what they want to know. Some publishers will want examples of your work, others prefer receiving an outline of an idea plus details of your background. Your covering letter should include details of any publishing history you might possess such as features you have written, or other books in which you have been involved. You should also highlight any relevant expertise you possess, such as teaching experience. If you are proposing a book about boats and the sea, then it might help if you mention that you enjoy messing about in boats or go scuba-diving in the ocean.

Some publishers still prefer would-be authors to send manuscripts by post with a covering letter plus an SAE if you want the manuscript returned.

Other publishers are quite happy to receive email submissions, or ask you to submit material via their website. If material is sent to a website, it often means that the publisher's final decision as to whether they are interested in your story or not, will depend on the reactions of visitors to the site and what they choose to read.

Yet others will only consider material submitted to them by agents.

> 'To find a publisher or agent, the best advice is to use the *Children's Writers' & Artists' Yearbook* published by Bloomsbury.'

Check out the exact address to which to send the material. Make sure you are sending it to the right person.

Agents

An agent is a go-between, a middleman who stands between the author and the publisher. Agents are always seeking manuscripts, looking for the next big children's author. Always remember that they are seeking people with whom they can have a long-term relationship, writers who are capable of writing more than one book, and more than one type of book.

When they receive a manuscript, it is read and assessed for publication value. They may provide comments and suggestions as to how it can be improved. They may say they would like to work with you and seek to get it published. If they do offer to represent you, then there will be long-term costs. They will charge around 10 to 15% of royalties.

For that money, they will work hard. A reputable agent knows what publishers are looking for and will be able to send the manuscript to the editors whom they believe will be most interested. Because the manuscript is coming from an agent, it will receive a higher rating within the publishing house. They know that the agent will only be providing manuscripts that are worth considering.

The agent may be able to provide you with extra sources of revenue. Publishers contact them with editorial briefs, saying they are looking for writers who can provide a particular type of stories. The agent then looks at the writers it represents, and contacts those writers whom the agent feels would be interested.

If a publisher decides to publish your work, the agent will negotiate on your behalf regarding royalties, advances, possible foreign rights (and who knows, perhaps even movie rights!). If problems occur, then the agent has to deal with them.

Much does depend on the agent and the relationship between agent and writer. A successful and happy relationship can be very rewarding – it takes a lot of the pressure off a writer. You may concentrate on doing what you do best – writing. The agent deals with number crunching, negotiating and finding publishers.

'Remember that an agent will be representing many writers and there is only a limited amount of time they can devote to you.'

But there can be problems. Remember that an agent will be representing many writers and there is only a limited amount of time they can devote to you. The relationship might not work – you may find you just do not get on with the agent on a personal basis. You may find you are getting more work yourself than the agent can provide. There may be jobs which the agent doesn't suggest because the fee is too low, especially flat fees.

Although flat fees for projects will not bring you much money in the long term, they can help get you started and get your name known. A successful one-off project can bring your name to the attention of other publishers.

Agents will only take on a handful of writers.

Ultimately it comes down to your own personal choice whether you choose the agent route or not.

The best way to find an agent is to look in the pages of *Children's Writers' and Artists' Yearbook.*

Checklist

- Make sure that the publisher or agent you have chosen actually publishes the type of book you have written.

- Make sure that it is presented to their requirements. Do they want material sent electronically, via a website, via an agent, or a hard copy in the post?

- All manuscripts should be typed, not handwritten. Use double spacing and number the pages.

- Send the manuscript to the correct address.

- Be professional and business-like in the way you send out a manuscript. Make sure the manuscript is tidy, well written, has no spelling mistakes and is grammatically correct.

Response from publishers

Having sent your manuscript off, what happens next? All you can do is wait and start writing or preparing your next book.

Do not expect instant reactions from a publisher. It can take three months or more for them to make up their minds. Sometimes they do not even answer. You may never hear from them.

Keep a list of the publishers and agents you have approached. This will make sure you do not send the same material to them twice. Note down what reaction you get.

Publication

If a publisher responds to your query, they may say yes we are interested, but would like these changes made. It is up to you to decide whether you want to go along with those changes and revise the manuscript. You may find having made those initial changes, they will come back with requests for yet more revisions until they are finally satisfied.

It is worth taking the time to meet their demands for revisions. They know their market and they are obviously interested in your work. If they were not interested, they would not be asking for revisions. Follow their advice and it will increase your chances of eventually being published.

The final proof copy will be sent to you prior to publication so that you can undertake a final check. This copy will contain pictures and page numbers. You need to check that everything is OK with the script. Usually there are no problems but occasionally errors can creep in – on one occasion I found that a picture was upside down.

You may be asked to provide an index. To do this, you need to list all the important topics and note down the pages on which they appear. The index should be created in alphabetical order, and all page references should be in number order.

Book cover

The cover is very important and a key part of the final editing process. The cover has to sum up what the book is about, and encourage potential readers to actually open the book and start reading. On a crowded bookshelf, a title can be easily overlooked – the cover helps the book to stand out and catch someone's attention.

'On a crowded bookshelf, a title can be easily overlooked – the cover helps the book to stand out and catch someone's attention.'

You will usually be sent two or three ideas for the cover. You will need to comment on these, and say which you prefer. You will probably not have the final say – the editor will be seeking other opinions from the sales department, the marketing department and other editors.

Payment

If your work is accepted, do not immediately give up your day job. Writing will not make you rich overnight. Making a living as a professional writer is hard work. You need to be able to undertake lots of different types of writing in order to survive.

Having signed a contract, you may be offered an advance on sales. This is unlikely to be very high for a first-time writer. Remember that whatever they pay you as an advance will eventually be taken out of your royalties. It is not extra cash.

'If your work is accepted, do not immediately give up your day job. Writing will not make you rich overnight.'

Royalties begin to be made when the book is published. Depending on the publisher, it may be anything from 5 to 10% of what the publisher gets from sales. You will receive an account of sales every six or twelve months, depending on the individual publisher's normal practice. When the advance has been covered, you will start getting those all-important royalty cheques.

If your book has been accepted by a book packager, you may simply get a flat fee. This means that you will receive payment on completion of the project – and that is it. You do not get any royalties. All copyright and all money generated from sales belong to the publisher.

Deadlines

When taking on new authors, publishers are looking for people who are able to write more than just one book. They are looking for writers who are professional, have good writing ability and can meet deadlines.

Deadlines are extremely important. It is no use saying that you will do it when you get round to it, or when you feel like writing. Even writer's block will not be an excuse – it is up to you to find ways of dealing with writer's block and providing the required amount of words and the required story at the requested time. Publishers will only give you one chance. If you miss a deadline without having a really, really good excuse you will not be used again. The only acceptable reasons for not meeting a deadline tend to be serious illness or a computer blowing up – but then you have to make sure that the revised deadline is met with time to spare.

Dealing with rejections

Be prepared for rejections. Every writer gets rejected at some point. What is important is the type of rejection and how you deal with it.

Eoin Colfer, author of the best-selling *Artemis Fowl* series, sent his first book to a publisher carefully stapled together and bound with a self-designed cover. He waited for a response – nothing ever arrived. He sent out more copies of the manuscript to other publishers. There were a few replies – all rejections. He then did some research and purchased a copy of the Writers' Guide. This enabled him to work out what he was doing wrong.

He wrote more stories including the first Artemis Fowl. This time when he submitted them to publishers – the answer was very positive!

You may get a note saying quite simply 'This story is not for us'.

Look carefully at rejection letters which give a reason why the story or non-fiction proposal has been rejected. It may be that you have sent it to the wrong publisher – it is not their type of book.

A rejection letter I once received gave me a lot of confidence. They said that they were rejecting the story because they had seen something similar overseas, but that my writing was good and that I should carry on. Being told that I had talent was extremely positive and helpful.

You may get a response saying 'This story is not right for us but please send us more examples of your work'. This is a very positive response and should be followed up quickly. Send them more examples, and keep in touch with them. It indicates that they are interested, they like your style of writing and want to encourage you.

Some publishers may say 'Thanks but it is not right for us just now. We will keep your details on file'. This type of response is particularly common among non-fiction or educational publishers. It may mean that they have just

'Be prepared for rejections. Every writer gets rejected at some point. What is important is the type of rejection and how you deal with it.'

commissioned similar books from other authors, or that they are not commissioning anything for the time being. It could be just bad timing – their list may be top heavy with books about cats and your proposed book on the subject would be just too much.

Sometimes this is just a polite way of saying no, and stopping you chasing them. They may not even keep your details. Even if they keep your name on file, you will be just one of many people. If you contact a publisher who has already rejected you, this must be with a new idea. Wait for two or three months, then send more ideas.

If there is no response at all, look carefully at your material. Ask yourself whether better presentation might help. Are there lots of spelling mistakes? Does it look untidy? Would a little more editing be helpful?

Is the storyline unoriginal? Publishers do not want stories that are similar to what is already available – they are looking for something new and different.

Above all, be persistent. Have a list of alternative publishers ready to use. If you get rejected – and you will – look at the reasons they give.

Resend material to another publisher quickly. It makes you feel a little better and gives you hope!

Keep trying. Send out new proposals and write more stories. Look for opportunities in competitions, short story collections and annuals – anything to start getting your name known and in print. If you can point to places where you have had work published, then publishers will start to look at you more favourably. Always remember that publishers want to make sure that you are serious about your writing and that you will finish what you begin.

Publishers are always wary of people new to them, even if they already have a track record elsewhere. This is because all of them will have had experience of commissioning work which is not up to standard, not the right word length and not delivered on time, if at all. This emphasises the crucial importance of meeting deadlines, and providing exactly what the publisher asks.

Talented new work will eventually find a market. The rise of e-books is making it cost-effective for new and existing publishers to publish new fiction that otherwise would be too much of a gamble on a printed book.

Checklist

- Expect to get rejections.
- Have a list of alternative publishers ready.
- Follow any advice you get given.
- Be persistent.
- Keep trying.

Competitions

These can be a good way of drawing attention to your work. Publishers do keep an eye on competition entries. Even if a particular entry does not win, it may arouse the interest of a publisher or agent.

Sometimes publishers set up competitions as a way of finding new authors. A good example of this is The Times/Chicken House Children's Fiction annual competition. Open to first-time writers of a full length novel suitable for children between the ages of 9 and 16; it offers a worldwide publishing contract to the winner. The winning entry is chosen by a panel of judges which includes children's authors, journalists, publishers and librarians.

Self publishing

This has always been an option for new writers and if you are planning on this route, choose carefully. There are different methods of self publishing — and not all will be successful.

Traditional vanity publishing is not well regarded by conventional mainstream publishers. Vanity publishers are easily found in the pages of magazines and newspapers. They advertise, asking for manuscripts. Bear in mind that reputable publishers never ask for manuscripts – they get plenty of material coming direct to them.

When a vanity publisher receives a manuscript, they invariably give you a flattering report and say millions of copies can be sold. They then demand very high sums of money to publish it. The quality of the publishing can be variable – and the costs high. You are funding the book. When the book is printed, you then have the task of marketing and selling the publication. It can take a lot of time and effort to make an income from this type of publishing – and it is rarely successful. If all you want to do is have self-written book with your name on the cover that you can sell to friends and family, then this method may be suitable. But bear in mind it can be very expensive.

A self-publishing company will not make excessive claims about sales or recouping your costs. They will usually point out that it is unlikely you will make a profit. They will provide a break down of their services, allowing you to choose which parts of their services you wish to use. You might, for example, choose to use their production and selling facilities, but undertake all the marketing yourself.

The Internet has made web-based publishing much easier. There are numerous systems such as PageMaker, Quark XPress which enable even a first-time writer to edit a manuscript into a reasonable format. You can then try selling direct from your own website as either an e-book, or as a print on demand service.

It must be said that sometimes self publishing can work. Writer G P Taylor is a Yorkshire vicar who sold his motorcycle to pay for the printing costs of his book *Shadowmancer*. It proved to be a runaway success. A mainstream publisher has since decided to publish *Shadowmancer* and its sequels. Another example is that of Christopher Paolini's *Eragon*. As a teenage boy, he wrote the book and self published it, selling copies to friends, family and local people. Word began to spread, and demand for copies soared. Eventually a major publisher came across the book, read it and offered a contract. This has resulted in worldwide sales, a series of books and the initial book even became a film.

Checklist

- Are you considering self publishing or vanity publishing?

- How much hard work are you prepared to put in to make it a success?

- How much money can you commit to the venture?

ISBN numbers

If you are self publishing, you will need an ISBN (International Standard Book Number) code. This is a 10-digit number which is used by publishers, booksellers and librarians when they order and list books. The numbers are divided into four parts:

Group identifier – This identifies the national, geographic or language grouping of a publisher.

Publisher identifier – The specific publisher or imprint.

Title number – Identifies the specific book in a specific format.

Check digit – This is the final digit which mathematically validates the rest of the number.

High street retailers and Internet retailers use the ISBN to keep track of books, deal with ordering and payment. Using an ISBN also provides access to bibliographic databases that are used by the book trade and libraries to provide information to customers. If your book is not listed on that database, then potential customers will not be able to track it.

ISBNs are assigned to publishers, including self publishers. A publisher is described as being the person who takes the risk in making a book available. If you are the person paying for the production of a book, and are responsible for its marketing, distribution and sales, then you are a publisher. A small fee is payable to the ISBN Agency. Contact www.isbn.nielsenbookdata.co.uk for more information.

ISBN numbers can only be purchased in blocks of 10. It is not possible to obtain just one ISBN number.

Elements of ISBN numbers can form part of a bar code used by retailers. The bar code does have to be obtained separately – contact the Book Industry Communication website www.bic.org.uk for more information.

Publicity

Whether you are being published or self publishing, be prepared for a lot of hard work. You need to contact everyone you know, friends, colleagues, organisations; contact booksellers, mail order businesses, Internet retailers and offer free readings at schools and libraries. Look for any opportunity to encourage sales and arouse interest.

Libraries are a very useful form of publicity. They frequently have discussion groups and hold events where authors can give talks. Reading a book from a library can encourage people to go out and buy it.

You will need to convince retailers to take your book and sell it. They will want to know how you are planning to publicise it, and whether you will be available to do book signings and promotional events. You will need to take copies to booksellers and other retailers and convince them that sales can be achieved. They will not buy it from you – sale or return is normal. As a self publisher you will also need to appoint a distributor. Choose a company which has contacts with the national chains. Take part in book festivals and other book events to ensure ongoing sales.

'Libraries are a very useful form of publicity.'

Publishers may ask you to provide information on local bookshops and possible places where the book could be sold. Local bookshops like to feature the work of local writers in their displays.

You will need to fill out a publicity questionnaire giving information about yourself. The publishers will use this as a basis for press releases and publicity information which are sent to journalists and book reviewers. If you are lucky, you may be asked to undertake interviews in person or by phone with magazines, local papers and radio stations. Don't expect an instant reaction. The press will not be running to your door asking for quotes and interviews. Unless there is a really good story involved, you are more likely to get involved in requests to participate in readings at libraries and schools or author signings in local bookshops. Schools workshops can be a good method of generating publicity – Jacqueline Wilson visited schools up to three times a week before her books really became famous.

Public lending rights

Encouraging libraries to stock your book will help publicity and ultimately your income. In 2012, children's writers were among the top 10 most popular authors in UK libraries. They were Daisy Meadows, the brand behind the *Rainbow Magic* series (2nd), Jacqueline Wilson (4th), Francesca Simon, author of the *Horrid Henry* series (5th) Julia Donaldson (7th) and Mick Inkpen (9th). The Public Lending Right Act of 1979 relates to all books loaned from public lending libraries. Authors can apply to go on a list operated by the PLR. An author must be able to prove that they are named on the title page or can prove authorship by other means such as being in receipt of royalties and provide relevant ISBN numbers. If your claim is accepted, then your name goes on the PLR list, enabling you to receive a share of the monies allotted by the government each year to the PLR fund. The exact amount each author receives depends on computerised estimates of loans credited to each requested book. The computer does this using ISBN numbers across a different selection of libraries each year.

UK authors can apply for PLR payments from Germany, Austria, Estonia, Ireland, The Netherlands, France, Belgium and Spain via ALCS. As other EU countries implement PLR schemes, ALCS will add these countries.

ALCS stands for Authors' Licensing and Collecting Society. It collects international payments and pays these out to authors twice a year. All types of writers can apply to join ALCS.

Writing a book is hard work but very rewarding. Simply creating a finished story is an achievement. Getting it published – and possibly getting an income from your work – is an even bigger achievement. Success does not come easily – you have to work for it, especially if you are opting for self publishing. Coping with rejections can be disheartening – but remember that every author, even well-known ones like Beatrix Potter and J K Rowling, has been turned down at some point in their career.

Whatever method of publication you choose to use, remember that it will not be instant money. It will take time – sometimes two years or more before you start seeing the results of your work. Don't give up the day job, and have patience.

A writer needs imagination, flexibility, ambition and patience to successfully bring a story to an end. It is important not to give up, even if you feel discouraged. Build up your files and information collections. Be a magpie and gather ideas and information wherever you can. Keep trying, and write more and more stories. Don't wait to achieve success with just one story – keep on writing, keep on looking for new ideas and new opportunities.

Good luck!

'Don't wait to achieve success with just one story – keep on writing, keep on looking for new ideas and new opportunities.'

Summing Up

- Be persistent and keep trying.

- Be prepared for rejections and be ready to deal with them.

- Look carefully at how you present your work.

- Follow publisher's guidelines.

- Do not expect instant success.

- Becoming a published writer takes time, effort, persistence and luck.

Glossary

ALCS

This is the Authors' Licensing and Collecting Society. It collects international payments and pays these out to authors twice a year. All types of writers can apply to join the ALCS.

Copyright

This is a property right which exists in almost every kind of work – written, printed, electronic, film, media, sound. Protection is automatic and gives control of the right of copying to the author or creator of a piece of work. For example this book is © Angela Youngman.

Copyright is a complex issue. Every country has its own copyright laws. At its simplest it refers to any written or drawn works which you create from your own imagination, or are the result of your own research and not undertaken on behalf of a company who has contracted you to do the work. You and your estate retain copyright during your lifetime, and 70 years after your death.

Genre

This is a category into which books can be divided, such as science fiction, crime, fantasy and horror.

ISBN

ISBN stands for International Standard Book Number. It is a number used by publishers, booksellers and librarians to identify books when ordering, listing and keep track of stock. Self publishers can acquire blocks of 10 ISBN numbers from www.isbn.nielsenbookdata.co.uk

Permission

If you want to reproduce sections of someone's work within your own book, you have to get their permission. You may have to pay for this. If you do not obtain the required permission, it can result in legal action. Simply mentioning an author's work, or referring to information about it which is in the public domain does not require permission.

PLR

Public lending right relates to all books loaned from public libraries. Many other countries are joining the UK in setting up a PLR system.

Proof copy

Prior to publication, publishers send the author a proof copy of the book for final checking. It will have page numbers on and any illustrations.

Royalties

The author's share of profits made from sales of a book. You may get paid an advance on royalties. This means you do not get paid any further royalties after publication, until that advance has been earned.

Help List

ACHUKA Children's Books UK

www.achuka.co.uk

A comprehensive online guide to children's book publishing. It highlights trends and includes many author interviews, plus book news from around the world.

BBC Education

www.bbc.co.uk/schools

A useful website if you are trying to find out about the UK schools' curriculum. It is a very good resource for anyone planning to write for educational publishers.

Children's Literature

www.childrenslit.com

A US database which contains reviews of children's books. It tries to be as comprehensive as possible and currently has over 400,000 reviews on its database. This is a useful way of spotting trends and getting information about books.

Children's Writers & Artists Yearbook

Bloomsbury Books

www.writersandartists.co.uk

This is an extremely useful book for any writer targeting the children's market. It contains listings for agents, publishers, magazines, newspapers, television and radio, as well as lots of useful information and advice from established writers.

National Curriculum Online

www.education.gov.uk

This is the official National Curriculum website. It contains the statutory curriculum followed by UK state schools, plus attainment targets for Key Stages 1 to 4.

Seven Stories, the Centre for Children's Books

www.sevenstories.org.uk

A unique centre for children's books with exhibitions, resource materials and a collection of manuscripts and artwork.

JacketFlap

www.jacketflap.com

A useful website allowing you to connect to the work of more than 200,000 authors, illustrators, publishers and other creators of books for children and young adults. You can read blogs and network with people in the industry including agents and illustrators.

Nielsen Bookdata

www.isbn.nielsenbookdata.co.uk

This is the website for the ISBN agency which allots numbers to new books. A registration fee has to be paid by all new publishers, and will give you a specific publisher prefix to be used as part of your ISBN number.

Society of Authors

www.societyofauthors.org

This is a useful organisation to which many authors belong. It was founded 100 years ago. Membership is available to authors who have had a full length book published and those authors who have had a full length book accepted. It has its own Children's Writers and Illustrators Group (CWIG) and an Educational Writers Group.

The Society of Authors sets out to further the interests of writers and artists, and defend them when necessary. It can provide information on agents, publishers and provide advice on negotiations with the different organisations and companies. It can help deal with queries which arise while negotiating contract details. The Society of Authors also holds regular conferences, seminars, meetings and social activities which provide a facility for networking.

Write4kids

www.write4kids.com

A US Internet site containing lots of articles and general information about writing children's books.

UK Children's books

www.ukchildrensbooks.co.uk
This is a directory of authors, illustrators and publishers involved with children's books and reading generally.

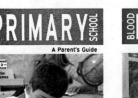

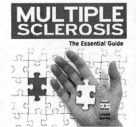